From the publisher of the popular *Tidewater on the Half Shell* comes another cookbook destined to make its own mark in the cookbook world.

Produced by the Junior League of Norfolk-Virginia Beach, Inc., *Toast to Tidewater* features recipes that share the ingredients and culinary delights of the Hampton Roads, Virginia, region.

The triple-tested recipes feature fresh ingredients, including peanuts, ham, pork, seafood, vegetables, fruit, and other fine products of Virginia. The recipes reflect the diversity of today's cook and are sophisticated and suitable for entertaining family and friends.

Since the first settlers arrived in Virginia in 1607, Virginia's wine industry has grown steadily. Over the past few decades, the industry has grown by leaps and bounds to become one of the nation's largest wine producers. *Toast to Tidewater* pays tribute to this industry by pairing over half of the recipes with Virginia wines, ciders, and beers.

Toast to Tidewater also tours the Hampton Roads region, an area rich in history, tradition, culture, and a passion for fresh, fabulous food.

Enjoy all the delights that make up *Toast to Tidewater*. And in the tradition of true Southern hospitality, be sure to share it with others!

Cover Photo Sponsor

Many thanks to *Farm Fresh Supermarkets* for their most generous sponsorship of the cover photograph.
Farm Fresh Supermarkets
—*When Only The Very Best Will Do!*

JUNIOR LEAGUE OF
NORFOLK-VIRGINIA BEACH, INC.

Women building better communities

The Junior League of Norfolk-Virginia Beach, Inc., is an organization of women committed to promoting voluntarism, developing the potential of women, and improving communities through effective action and leadership of trained volunteers. Its purpose is exclusively educational and charitable.

The Junior League of Norfolk-Virginia Beach, Inc.
Norfolk, Virginia
Copyright © 2004 by the Junior League of Norfolk-Virginia Beach, Inc.
Photographs copyright © 2004 by Mark Edward Atkinson
Illustrations copyright © 2004 by Lee Walker Shepherd
All rights reserved.
First Edition: 10,000 copies September 2004
Second Edition: 10,000 copies March 2005
Printed in the United States of America
Production and manufacturing by Teagle and Little, Inc.

This cookbook is a collection of favorite recipes
which are not necessarily original recipes.

Library of Congress Catalog-in-Publication Data
Main entry under title:
Toast to Tidewater, *Celebrating Virginia's Finest Food & Beverages*
2004107147

ISBN: 0-9614767-1-0

Text by Junior League of Norfolk, Virginia Beach, Inc.
Designed by Lee Walker Shepherd
Typesetting by Lee Walker Shepherd

Also by the Junior League of Norfolk-Virginia Beach, Inc.:
Tidewater on the Half Shell (1985)

Any inquiries about *Toast to Tidewater* or orders
for additional copies should be directed to:
Toast to Tidewater
Junior League of Norfolk-Virginia Beach, Inc.
Post Office Box 956
Norfolk, VA 23501
(757) 623-7270
(866) 905-5682
www.jlnvb.org

Toast to Tidewater

CELEBRATING VIRGINIA'S FINEST FOOD & BEVERAGES

Junior League of Norfolk-Virginia Beach, Inc.

Art Direction & Design by Lee Walker Shepherd
Photography by Mark Edward Atkinson

APPETIZERS:

Toasting Occasion–Day of Firsts
Featuring Marinated Lemon Garlic Olives
Training and leadership are the strong foundations of Junior Leagues. The Junior League of Norfolk-Virginia Beach, Inc. Past Presidents proudly underwrite this photograph for the appetizer section to lead off the book — an expression of their lasting commitment to leadership and the League.

BRUNCH & BREADS:

Toasting Occasion–Love and Kisses
Featuring Brie Strata with Pungo Salsa
In honor of their commitment to voluntarism and improving communities around them, the photograph for the brunches and breads section is dedicated to all Active and Provisional members of the Association of Junior Leagues International, Inc.

SOUPS, SALADS & SANDWICHES:

Toasting Occasion–New Additions
Featuring Virginia Bouillabaisse
from The Williamsburg Winery
In honor of their continued service to helping those in need, the photograph for this section is dedicated to the numerous community-based organizations the Junior League of Norfolk-Virginia, Inc. partners with, including F.O.R. Kids, Inc. and Edmarc Hospice for Children, with whom we served during the production of this book.

PASTA:

Toasting Occasion–Family Gatherings
Featuring Artichoke & Onion Pasta
Hampton Roads Magazine, "The City and lifestyle magazine of Hampton Roads," has generously underwritten this photograph.

MEATS (BEEF, PORK & POULTRY):

Toasting Occasion–Welcome Home
Featuring Veal Chops with Grape Chutney
from Barboursville Vineyards
A grand assortment of history and culture exists in the 12 cities defined in this book as the Tidewater/Hampton Roads area and the photograph for this section is dedicated in their honor.

SEAFOOD:

Toasting Occasion–Don't Be Crabby, Another Year Younger
Featuring Buckroe Beach Soft Shell Crabs
Farm Fresh Supermarkets has generously underwritten this section photograph in addition to the cover photograph. *"Farm Fresh Supermarkets—When Only The Very Best Will Do!"*

VEGETABLES & SIDE DISHES:

Toasting Occasion–Give a Cheer
Featuring Eggplant Stuffed Peppers
Cheers to the wine panel mentioned on pages 156-157 for accomplishing a monumental task of pairing the recipes with Virginia wines, beers, and ciders for this book. The photograph for this section is dedicated in honor of their time, patience, and expertise.

DESSERTS:

Toasting Occasion–Holiday Charm
Featuring Berry Tart with Mascarpone Cream
The Junior League of Norfolk-Virginia Beach, Inc., Sustaining members have generously underwritten this section photograph. The charm and charisma of these women bring truth to the old adage, "save the best for last."

Contents

PROFESSIONAL CREDITS
& ACKNOWLEDGEMENTS

ART DIRECTION
PHOTO CONCEPTS
DESIGN & ILLUSTRATION
Lee Walker Shepherd

PHOTOGRAPHY
Mark Edward Atkinson

PREPARED FOOD
PHOTO & FOOD STYLING
Tracey Lee
Lee Walker Shepherd

RECIPE CONSULTING
Chef John Cappellucci,
Tidewater Community College
PJ Forbes,
Cookbook Consultant

MENU CREATION
Sigrid Couch

COPY EDITOR
Maureen O'Driscoll

CONTENT EDITOR
Bill Bailey

PRINT PRODUCTION
Teagle & Little Printing

PHOTOGRAPHY PROPS & DISHWARE
Provided by
Donna Marie Murphy, *Le Marche*
Tracey Lee
Lee Walker Shepherd

Special Thanks

The JLNVB extends a sincere thank you to:
Jack Shepherd, Bill Forbes, Trent Dudley, Ed Blair,
Dave Glovier, King Turgeon, Jeff Bowab, Anthony
Vittone, and all other spouses and family members
of the *Toast to Tidewater* committee members.
Without their love and support, this project would
not have been possible.

Foreword

"I'd like to propose a toast." We use this phrase to celebrate many special occasions—including weddings, anniversaries, reunions, and promotions—and we can think of no better toasting occasion than the completion of *Toast to Tidewater, Celebrating Virginia's Finest Food and Beverages.* Many people—League members and non-League members alike—have poured countless hours into developing, testing, planning, designing, writing, editing, and promoting this cookbook.

Toast to Tidewater builds on the strong foundation established by our first cookbook, *Tidewater on the Half Shell.* This award-winning, classic book of simple elegance and timeless recipes has served the Junior League of Norfolk-Virginia Beach, Inc. well.   Now, nearly 20 years later, we've created a fresh and new book that puts a creative twist on both modern and traditional flavors indigenous to our region.   The recipes in *Toast to Tidewater* are as good and reliable as those in *Tidewater on the Half Shell* because of testing and refinement by our talented League members.

As any good cook knows, a great recipe begins with different ingredients that work together to create a distinctive and wonderful taste. Two cups of this, three tablespoons of that, a dash of salt—all combine to create a recipe that satisfies our culinary cravings. Just like a recipe, the committees and members that worked on this project had a special blend of talents and skills—all extraordinary, all important. Everyone's contributions, no matter how small, were essential to the success of this effort. This cookbook serves as a tribute to these individuals and their dedication to the community in which they serve.

Toast to Tidewater also pays tribute to the Commonwealth of Virginia's fast-growing wine and beverage industry. When the first settlers arrived in Virginia in 1607, they recognized the potential of the first grapes produced. Over the past few decades, the Virginia wine industry has grown by leaps and bounds to become one of the nation's largest wine producers. This cookbook pairs more than half of its recipes with a Virginia wine, cider, or beer selected by a panel of seven wine experts.

As the Tidewater area is the first permanent English settlement in America, residents are proud of its history and heritage. This book also showcases 12 cities that make up Tidewater—highlighting its history, traditions, culture, and landmarks.

We salute *Toast to Tidewater* and all the wonderful folks who made it possible. We hope that you will enjoy using this cookbook as much as we enjoyed publishing it. May you use it to create and share great meals and great moments with family and friends. Cheers!

Committee

PROJECT & COMMITTEE CHAIRS:
Sally Dudley 2002-2004
Amy Cobb 2003-2004
Julie Yutesler 2002-2003

SUSTAINING ADVISORS:
PJ Forbes, Project Development & Recipe Consultant 2001-2004
Lee Walker Shepherd, Art Director 2002-2004
Paige Romig, Sponsorship 2003-2004

SUB COMMITTEE CHAIRS 2003-2004:
Sarah Bailey, Creative Design Research & Copy Writing
Tricia Blair, Sponsorship
Cami Glovier, Creative Design Research & Copy Writing
Kristina Smith, Wine Pairing, Research & Copy Writing
Elizabeth Vittone, Marketing

2003-2004 PRODUCTION:

Tracy Austgen, Recipe Editing
Susan Dixon, Sponsorship
Shann Johnson, Sponsorship
Ingrid McGowan, Marketing
Sunny Mueller, Marketing
Ann Pavilack, Recipe Index
Ashley Plumb, Creative Design Research & Copy Writing

Allison Rachels, Sponsorship Special Events
Kim Schrantz, Sponsorship
Christine Verfurth, Creative Design Research & Copy Writing
Susanne Vigus, Sponsorship
Anne Whipp, Creative Design Research & Copy Writing
Flurry Yanez, Sponsorship

PROJECT SUPPORTERS 2003-2004:

Joy Bixler
Kristan Burch
Molly Dey
Katherine Knaus
Ann Morgan
Mary Opitz

Dawn Peters
Jacqueline Peters
Martha Raiss
Kathy Shelton
Melissa Siemens
Ilona Webb-Bruner

COOKBOOK CHAIRS:
Amy Cobb, Chair & Barrett Bussard, Chair-Elect 2004-2005

**2002-2003
RECIPE TESTING
& RESEARCH DEVELOPMENT**
Page Allard
Nida Antonio
Sarah Bailey
Tricia Blair
Margie Chapman
Kim Chope
Amy Cobb
Leslie Councill
Francine Deir
Cami Glovier
Nicole Michelon
Sara Moriarty
Stacy Parker
Ann Pavilack
Nicole Powell
Beth Ripa
Amy Schabot
Kristina Smith
Eleanor Trickler
Elizabeth Vittone
Anne Whipp

**2001-2002
RECIPE COLLECTION
& THEME CREATION**
Blair Ellson, Co-Chair
Gray Lawson, Co-Chair
Page Allard
Tricia Blair
Shelly Brown
Tamara DeGraw
Jenn Demmin
Rebecca Frith
Laurie Harrison
Ginny Hawley
Vicky Hecht
Tracey Martin
Julie McConahy
Carter McKay
Sara Moriarty
Beth Ripa
Cynthia Sabol
Cindy Sherwood
Laura Wheeler
Lisa Williams
Flurry Yanez
Julie Yutesler

•Williamsburg

•Jamestown   Yorktown•

CHESAPEAKE BAY

Poquoson•

•Newport News

Hampton•

Smithfield•

HAMPTON ROADS

ATLANTIC
OCEAN

N

•Norfolk

Portsmouth•

Virginia Beach•

Franklin•   Suffolk•

Chesapeake•

Introduction

WHAT'S IN A NAME?

Where in Virginia is Tidewater? Where exactly is Hampton Roads? Is Tidewater in Hampton Roads? Or is Hampton Roads, in fact, part of Tidewater? These questions have long perplexed and confounded residents and nonresidents alike. Often the terms are used interchangeably. The following discussion provides some insight into these regional designations. Whether you call it Tidewater or Hampton Roads, one thing is certain: The area is rich in culture and history and its culinary delights are plentiful.

Hampton Roads is one of the top 30 largest Metropolitan Statistical Areas (MSA) in the United States as designated by the Federal Office of Management and Budget. The region is noted as the area where three Virginia rivers converge—the James, Nansemond, and Elizabeth—and open into the Chesapeake Bay. Hampton Roads has 1.5 million residents and comprises the cities of Chesapeake, Franklin, Hampton, Newport News, Norfolk, Poquoson, Portsmouth, Suffolk, Virginia Beach, and Williamsburg. The counties of Gloucester, Isle of Wight (Smithfield), James City, Mathews, Southampton, Surry, and York (Yorktown) are also included in what is defined as Hampton Roads. The MSA is also inclusive of Currituck County, North Carolina.

The name "Hampton Roads" has historic ties to the seventeenth century English Earl of Southampton, Henry Wirothesley. The area was named in the Earl's honor by the first royal governor in the early 1600s. In nautical terms, "road" means a protected anchorage or a safe harbor. Hampton Roads' ports have served shipping interests and mariners worldwide for nearly 400 years.

According to the Hampton Roads Chamber of Commerce, Hampton Roads has been designated as the "world's largest natural harbor" since the late seventeenth century. Its natural beauty, waterfront landscape, thriving maritime industry, and flourishing communities gracefully merge with its historic prominence, state-of-the-art technology, economic prosperity, and long-standing military presence.

The Hampton Roads region is often referred to as the Tidewater area—another designation with historic roots and varied meanings. To an astronomer or perhaps a mariner, tidewater is a coastal area whose streams are affected by the rise and fall of the ocean and bay tides and whose water is brackish. Geologically speaking, tidewater can also refer to the area east of the fall line of the rivers. For Tidewater, Virginia, this fall line can be approximated by Interstate 95. Virginia historian Charles A. Grymes notes that, to Virginia's southeastern residents, Tidewater is a "region with a complex mix of jurisdictions." The multiple waterways fragment the communities, and there is no "center" to the region. The borders of Tidewater are amorphous—communities are developed right against each other, making it difficult to identify boundaries of the encompassing cities and counties.

Anything the area may lack in centralization (which many residents find to be an asset), it more than makes up for with its outstanding quality of life, moderate seasonal climate, and affordable cost of living. The area has received accolades as one of the best regions in which to raise a family and also as one of the fittest cities in the United States. Its numerous waterways provide not only beautiful scenery but also enhance the growing economy.

So whether you refer to the area as Tidewater or Hampton Roads, it matters not—the Junior League of Norfolk-Virginia Beach, Inc., is a proud member of the encompassing communities. The Junior League uses both terms to refer to the area, but from a cookbook and culinary perspective, we have consistently designated the region as Tidewater—first in our award-winning *Tidewater on the Half Shell* and now in our current endeavor. So please enjoy our *Toast to Tidewater*!

Day of Firsts Menu

(First car, First house, First steps, First job)

◆

Marinated Lemon Garlic Olives

Savory Rosemary Almonds

Spicy Shrimp & Crab Bruschetta

Pair with The Williamsburg Winery Acte 12 Chardonnay or

Rockbridge Vineyard DeChiel Pinot Noir

◆

Pork Tenderloin with Williamsburg Porter™ & Cherry Demi-Glace

Rosemary Roasted Potato & Fennel Hash

Mixed Greens dressed with Tidewater Dressing

Pair with Horton Cellars Winery Stonecastle White

◆

Chocolate Butterfinger® Crème Brulee

Pair with La Provencale Cellars Le Mousseaux Sparkling Virginia Cider

or Barboursville Vineyards Sangiovese Reserve

Section photograph underwritten by:
JLNVB Past Presidents

*Here's to change.
May it always be the improvement you've dreamed of.
Here's to newness.
May it always feel special but comfortable.
Here's to beginnings.
May your special first never be your last.*

—Toast written by Anne McPhee, JLNVB member

Marinated Lemon Garlic Olives

Advance preparation required.

Serves **6**
Preparation time: 15 minutes

Can be served in martini glasses and
makes a great hostess or holiday gift.

1 jar (10 ounces) pimento stuffed olives, divided
4 sprigs fresh oregano, divided
3 cloves garlic, pressed, divided
2 lemons thinly sliced, divided
10 black peppercorns, divided
3 tablespoons lemon juice

TO MAKE OLIVES:

◆ Drain olives and reserve liquid.
◆ Layer half of olives, half of oregano, half of garlic, half of lemon
  slices, and half of peppercorns in a 3-cup container.
◆ Repeat layers with remaining olives, oregano, garlic, lemon slices, and
  peppercorns.
◆ Pour lemon juice over olive layers.
◆ Add enough reserve olive liquid to fill container.
◆ Place lid on container.
◆ Chill for at least eight hours.
◆ Store in refrigerator up to two weeks.

Asparagus Delights

Advance preparation required.

Serves 6
Preparation time: 20 minutes

A delightful spring appetizer or first course.

1 pound fresh asparagus, cooked
3 ounces prosciutto, thinly sliced into 6 strips
6 tablespoons Boursin™ cheese
1/3 cup olive oil
1/4 cup balsamic vinegar
1/4 cup dry red wine
1/2 cup pine nuts, toasted

TO MAKE ASPARAGUS:

◆ Let asparagus cool from cooking.
◆ Place 1 strip of prosciutto on each of six plates.
◆ Divide and place asparagus evenly on top of prosciutto.
◆ Place 1 tablespoon of Boursin™ cheese in middle of each group of asparagus.
◆ The asparagus can be held covered in the refrigerator for several hours until ready to be served.
◆ Stir together olive oil, balsamic vinegar, and red wine in a saucepan; bring to a boil.
◆ Remove olive oil mixture from heat and let cool at room temperature for 20–30 minutes.
◆ Pour cooled olive oil mixture over asparagus when ready to serve.
◆ Sprinkle with pine nuts and serve immediately.

Baked Wild Mushrooms with Basil & Garlic

Serves 4
Preparation time: 20 minutes
Cooking time: 40 minutes

This is also a great side dish with a meat entrée.

1 head garlic
1½ pounds white button, shiitake, or cremini mushrooms, halved or quartered if large
1 medium shallot, thinly sliced
1/3 cup extra virgin olive oil or basil flavored oil
Salt and freshly ground black pepper
10–15 basil leaves, thinly sliced
Crusty bread

TO MAKE MUSHROOMS:

◆ Preheat oven to 400 degrees.
◆ Break garlic into individual cloves.
◆ Trim off garlic points, peel, and cut in half.
◆ Mix garlic cloves, mushrooms, shallots, and olive oil in a single layer of a roasting pan just large enough to hold all the ingredients; salt and pepper to taste.
◆ Bake, stirring every 10 minutes, until the mushrooms and garlic are browned and tender, approximately 40 minutes.
◆ Stir in the basil leaves during the last 10 minutes.
◆ Serve warm with crusty bread.

Calling all history buffs. When you enter the Tidewater area, you've hit an American history jackpot. From the first permanent English settlement to the last major battle of the American Revolutionary War, you can see and experience history firsthand by visiting the Jamestown Settlement and the Yorktown Victory Center.

Travel back in time to 1607 and the founding of the Jamestown Settlement, the first permanent English settlement in the New World. There you'll learn about the people of seventeenth century Virginia, including the Powhatan Indians, European colonists, and African slaves. In recreated settings, costumed historic interpreters illustrate what life may have been like three and four centuries ago. A Powhatan Indian village, a colonial fort, and replicas of the Susan Constant, Godspeed, and Discovery—the ships that transported English settlers—provide living history at its best.

At the Yorktown Victory Center, you'll discover the lives of men and women who witnessed the American Revolution and the formation of the new nation. A Revolutionary War encampment and 1780s farm are yours to learn from and explore. There you can don a soldier's uniform, join the Continental Army, or help out with colonial farm chores.

A visit to Jamestown and Yorktown proves that history is never boring when it is experienced firsthand.

Coastal Crab & Brie Bites

Yields **18**
Preparation time: 15 minutes
Cooking time: 5 minutes

A great traveling recipe.

8 ounces Brie cheese, rind removed
(freeze Brie cheese slightly to make removal of rind easier)
¼ cup heavy cream
¼ teaspoon Old Bay® seasoning
2 teaspoons dry sherry
1 cup fresh backfin crabmeat
18 mini phyllo cups
2 tablespoons chopped fresh chives

TO MAKE APPETIZER:

◆ Preheat oven to 350 degrees.
◆ Cut Brie cheese into small pieces and place in a saucepan.
◆ Pour heavy cream over Brie cheese over low heat.
◆ Let Brie cheese melt completely, stirring occasionally.
◆ Stir Old Bay® seasoning and dry sherry into Brie mixture; mix thoroughly.
◆ Stir crabmeat gently into Brie mixture, until crabmeat is thoroughly covered.
◆ Place 1 tablespoon of crab and Brie mixture into each phyllo cup.
◆ Place in preheated 350 degree oven when all cups are full.
◆ Bake for five minutes.
◆ Remove from oven.
◆ Sprinkle with chives (for added color, dash tops with Old Bay® seasoning).

Fabulous Pesto-Feta Spread

Serves **8**
Preparation time: 20 minutes
Cooking time: 20 minutes

*You'll be the most popular hostess
with this incredible dish,
which is also a great omelet stuffer.*

8 ounces cream cheese, softened
2 ounces grated Parmesan cheese
½ cup basil pesto sauce
5 roma tomatoes, diced
½ cup chopped red onion
½ cup crumbled Feta cheese

TO MAKE SPREAD:

◆ Preheat oven to 350 degrees.
◆ Spray shallow 2-cup oval baking dish with cooking spray.
◆ Mix cream cheese and Parmesan cheese; stir in pesto; mix well.
◆ Stir in roma tomatoes and red onion; mix well.
◆ Place mixture in prepared baking dish.
◆ Sprinkle top of tomato mixture with Feta cheese.
◆ Bake in preheated 350 degree oven for 20 minutes or until bubbly.
◆ Serve with crackers or baguette.

Elegant Pesto Torte

Advance preparation required.

Serves 18
Preparation time: 60 minutes

Beautiful presentation with outstanding flavor.
Definitely worth the effort!

16 ounces cream cheese, softened
6 ounces goat cheese
2 cloves garlic, minced
6 teaspoons minced fresh oregano
$\frac{1}{8}$ teaspoon ground pepper
$\frac{1}{2}$ cup sun-dried tomatoes in oil, drained and chopped
$\frac{1}{2}$ cup chopped artichoke
$\frac{1}{2}$ cup finely chopped hearts of palm
$\frac{3}{4}$ cup prepared pesto
1 sun-dried tomato, sliced
2 tablespoons toasted slivered almonds
Fresh oregano sprigs and fresh parsley sprigs for garnish

TO MAKE TORTE:

◆ Beat cream cheese, goat cheese, garlic, oregano, and pepper at medium speed with an electric mixer until smooth.
◆ Mix sun-dried tomato, artichoke, and hearts of palm in a separate bowl.
◆ Line a soufflé dish with plastic wrap.
◆ Spread one-third of cream cheese mixture over the bottom of soufflé dish.
◆ Spread pesto evenly over cream cheese mixture.
◆ Spread half of remaining cream cheese mixture over the pesto layer.
◆ Spread all of the sun-dried tomato mixture over the cream cheese layer.
◆ Spread with remaining cream cheese mixture.
◆ Cover and chill in the refrigerator for several hours or overnight.
◆ Uncover torte and invert onto a serving platter; remove plastic wrap.
◆ Arrange sun-dried tomato slices on top.
◆ Press almonds against sides to cover.
◆ Garnish if desired with fresh oregano or parsley sprigs.
◆ Serve with melba toast, pita toast, crackers, baguettes, or fruit.

Champagne Fondue

Serves 10
Preparation time: 20 minutes

An elegant combination of flavors for an evening of charm and sophistication.

7 ounces Emmentaler cheese, shredded
14 ounces Gruyére cheese, shredded
4 teaspoons cornstarch
1 cup Champagne or sparkling wine
1 tablespoon lemon juice
¼ teaspoon nutmeg
French bread, cubed
Cooked shrimp
Smoked sausage
Raw vegetables (carrots, broccoli, etc.)

TO MAKE FONDUE:

◆ Mix Emmentaler and Gruyére cheeses in saucepan with cornstarch; add Champagne and lemon juice.

◆ Cook over medium heat, stirring constantly, until all the cheese is melted.

◆ Stir in nutmeg.

◆ Pour melted cheese into fondue pot; adjust heat to keep cheese warm and melted.

◆ Serve with chunks of bread, cooked shrimp, smoked sausage, or raw vegetables.

Classic Scotch & Soda Fondue

Serves 6
Preparation time: 25 minutes

The scotch adds a wonderful flavor to an old favorite.

1 clove garlic
16 ounces Cheddar cheese, shredded
1 tablespoon flour
5½ tablespoons scotch whisky
½ to ¾ cup club soda
1 teaspoon Worcestershire sauce
¼ tablespoon butter, melted
1 egg, lightly beaten
French bread, cubed

TO MAKE FONDUE:

◆ Rub inside of fondue pot with garlic clove.

◆ Place Cheddar cheese in a plastic bag; sprinkle flour over Cheddar cheese; shake bag to coat Cheddar cheese with flour.

◆ Place coated Cheddar cheese in a double boiler over simmering water, stirring constantly until all of Cheddar cheese is melted.

◆ Stir in scotch whisky, club soda (add only as much club soda as needed; you want the cheese to slowly drip from a spoon), Worcestershire sauce, and butter into cheese mixture; mix until smooth.

◆ Take a small amount of melted cheese in a separate dish and add to the beaten egg; mix well.

◆ Stir cheese and egg back into double boiler and blend.

◆ Pour cheese mixture into fondue pot.

◆ Serve with cubed loaves of thick-crusted bread.

Naked Mountain's Smoked Salmon Mousse

Advance preparation required.

Serves 8
Preparation time: 20 minutes

Serve with Naked Mountain Vineyard Chardonnay and water biscuits.

12 ounces smoked salmon, divided
1 tablespoon brandy
Juice of ½ lemon
16 ounces cream cheese, softened
4 ounces heavy cream
3 tablespoons finely chopped red onion
1 teaspoon fresh dill weed
White pepper to taste

TO MAKE MOUSSE:

- Place 11 ounces of smoked salmon, brandy, and lemon juice in a food processor.
- Process until smooth.
- With processor running, slowly add cream cheese and heavy cream.
- Process until smooth, but do not over process.
- Transfer mixture to a bowl.
- Chop remaining salmon.
- Mix red onion, dill weed, white pepper, and remaining salmon.
- Stir red onion mixture into salmon-cream cheese mixture; mix thoroughly.
- Place in a serving bowl and refrigerate several hours before serving.

Savory Rosemary Almonds

Yields 2 cups
Preparation time: 10 minutes
Cooking time: 30 minutes

4 tablespoons butter
2 tablespoons finely minced fresh rosemary
1 teaspoon kosher salt
¼ teaspoon cayenne pepper
½ teaspoon garlic powder
2 cups almonds

TO MAKE ALMONDS:

- Melt butter in a skillet over low heat.
- Stir rosemary, kosher salt, cayenne pepper, and garlic powder into melted butter.
- Remove butter mixture from the heat and let sit for 30 minutes.
- Preheat oven to 300 degrees.
- Stir and coat almonds with butter spice mixture.
- Line a baking sheet with heavy-duty aluminum foil.
- Place almonds coated with butter mixture in a single layer on aluminum foil.
- Bake in preheated 300 degree oven for 30 minutes, stirring nuts every 10 minutes.
- Let cool.
- Store in an airtight container.

In the Tidewater area, when you think of downtown, you think of Norfolk. Downtown Norfolk is a vibrant place to work, live, and visit. Many people call it the best-kept secret on the East Coast. Located on the Elizabeth River, the downtown area thrives on activities on or near its beautiful waterfront.

From April to October, one area of Norfolk's waterfront—known as Town Point Park—is alive with outdoor concerts and festivals. Next door to the park is Waterside, home to many restaurants, bars, and dance clubs. Even in the winter, the city is awash in festive lights and holiday decorations. The area brightens people's spirits with "Holidays in the City," which includes a Grand Illumination parade and runs from the days just before Thanksgiving through the first of January.

Downtown Norfolk is a mix of old and new. Nestled among historic office buildings and other landmarks are a shopping mall, quaint condominiums, and museums such as the Chrysler Museum of Art. After hours, the city comes alive on Granby Street, where there are plenty of restaurants and clubs to visit. For those who fancy sports, nearby Harbor Park boasts a beautiful baseball park as home to the Norfolk Tides. Hockey enthusiasts can catch the Norfolk Admirals playing at Scope.

As home to the largest and most powerful naval base in the world, Norfolk's strong ties to the Navy are evident all around downtown. The U.S.S. Wisconsin is berthed on the waterfront, serving as a powerful reminder of the many sacrifices made by our military.

(continued on following page)

Virginia Wontons

Yields **60**
Preparation time: 65 minutes
Cooking time: 5–9 minutes

Wontons can be prepared two hours in advance and held covered in the refrigerator.

WONTON FILLING

½ pound raw shrimp, shelled and deveined
½ pound raw ground pork
⅓ cup chopped green onion
¼ cup chopped fresh ginger
2 tablespoons soy sauce
1 tablespoon seasoned rice wine vinegar
1 teaspoon cornstarch
½ teaspoon salt
½ teaspoon pepper
1 package (14 ounces) wonton wrappers
Peanut oil

DIPPING SAUCE

4 tablespoons soy sauce
1 teaspoon grated fresh ginger
A few drops of sesame oil
1 green onion, sliced into fine rings

TO MAKE FILLING:

◆ Finely chop raw shrimp until ground; transfer to a large bowl.

◆ Stir in raw ground pork, onion, and ginger; mix thoroughly.

◆ Stir in soy sauce, rice wine vinegar, cornstarch, salt, and pepper; mix thoroughly.

◆ The mixture can be held covered in the refrigerator for two hours until ready to make the wontons.

TO FORM WONTONS:

◆ Set up a "square" for your workspace: filling, stack of wrappers, a small bowl of water, and a plate to receive wontons.

◆ Gather a rounded teaspoon of filling in one hand.

◆ In the other hand, peel off a wrapper from the stack, and place filling on wrapper approximately 1 inch from the top of the wrapper.

◆ Dot a finger in the water, and spread a thin line of moisture across the edges of the wrapper.

◆ Roll top of wrapper over filling and continue tightly rolling wrapper to the end.

◆ Press ends of wrapper with a wet finger to seal in filling; repeat with wrapper seam running from side to side.

◆ Place wonton on your receiving plate, and repeat the process for remaining wontons.

◆ Place wontons on wax paper sprayed with nonstick cooking spray and store in an airtight container.

◆ Cook wontons just before serving.

◆ Pour ½ inch of peanut oil into a large cast iron skillet over medium heat; bring oil to 325 degrees.

Continued on next page...

continued from page 16:

- Place wontons in peanut oil and cook; do not crowd wontons in skillet.
- Turn wontons often until golden brown, approximately two minutes.
- Remove wontons with a slotted spoon; serve immediately.
- Make dipping sauce while wontons are cooking.

TO MAKE SAUCE:

- Mix soy sauce, ginger, sesame oil, and green onions.
- Ladle into individual bowls for serving.

Spicy Shrimp & Crab Bruschetta

Serves **6**
Preparation time: 25 minutes
Cooking time: 12 minutes

Can be prepared six hours ahead—just cover and chill.

¼ cup clam juice
6 ounces uncooked large shrimp, peeled, and deveined
3 green onions, thinly sliced
⅓ cup mayonnaise
1 tablespoon fresh lemon juice
½ teaspoon paprika
¼ teaspoon cayenne pepper
4 ounces fresh crabmeat
Salt and pepper to taste
½ baguette, cut diagonally into ⅓ inch thick slices
3 tablespoons olive oil

TO MAKE BRUSCHETTA:

- Bring clam juice to boil in medium saucepan.
- Stir in shrimp, and reduce heat to medium; cover and cook just until shrimp are opaque in center, approximately two minutes.
- Remove shrimp from liquid with a slotted spoon, transfer to cutting board, and cool.
- Coarsely chop shrimp.
- Mix green onions, mayonnaise, lemon juice, paprika, and cayenne pepper in medium bowl.
- Carefully mix shrimp and crabmeat into green onion mixture; season with salt and pepper.
- Preheat oven to 375 degrees.
- Brush both sides of baguette slices lightly with oil; arrange in single layer on baking sheet.
- Bake in preheated 375 degree oven for approximately 10 minutes or until bread is golden.
- Cool baguette and mound shrimp mixture on top bread.
- Place on platter and serve.

In the small yet quaint community of Phoebus, just a short drive from downtown Hampton, is the home of Fort Monroe and the Chamberlain Hotel. Originally built to protect the entrance to Hampton Roads and the several port cities that had access to its waters, the fort now serves as the home of the Army's Training and Doctrine Command. Completed in 1834 and surrounded entirely by a moat, the star-shaped fort is the largest stone fortress in the United States.

Visitors to this historic site can tour the Casemate Museum and learn about the important role of Fort Monroe and the surrounding area in battles, wars, and the defense of Tidewater and about the famous persons who once walked the halls within the cases. One casemate was used as the prison cell for former Confederate President Jefferson Davis, while other casemates served as living quarters for soldiers and their families during World War II. Robert E. Lee and Edgar Allan Poe were also among those stationed here at one time. Visitors are sure to get an excellent history lesson as well as a spectacular view of the Chesapeake Bay.

Adjacent to Fort Monroe sits the grand old Chamberlain Hotel at Old Point Comfort. This privately-owned hotel also enjoys a commanding view of the Chesapeake Bay. With a historic tale of its own, the first hotel to occupy this spot was built in 1820. After serving as a hospital during the Civil War, the Hygeia Hotel was torn down and another hotel, which would become the Chamberlain, was built in its place.

(continued on following page)

Baked Wine & Cheese with Bread

Serves 4
Preparation time: 10 minutes
Cooking time: 20 minutes

Great to freeze and use another time.

3 tablespoons white wine
½ cup milk
1 teaspoon dry mustard
1 teaspoon garlic powder
5 slices day old French bread, 2 inches thick
3 ounces Swiss cheese, grated
3 ounces Havarti cheese, grated

TO MAKE APPETIZER:

◆ Preheat oven to 400 degrees.
◆ Spray a small baking dish with olive oil cooking spray.
◆ Mix wine, milk, dry mustard, and garlic powder in a shallow bowl.
◆ Stir to mix ingredients and dissolve mustard.
◆ Dip French bread in the liquid.
◆ Squeeze out excess liquid.
◆ Cut French bread into cubes.
◆ Line prepared baking dish with half of bread cubes.
◆ Place half of the cheeses on top of the bread cubes.
◆ Place remaining bread cubes on top of cheese.
◆ Sprinkle remaining cheeses over bread.
◆ Bake in preheated 400 degree oven for 20 minutes.
◆ Serve immediately with crackers.

Oasis Winery's Mushroom Points

Serves 6
Preparation time: 15 minutes

4 tablespoons butter, divided
8 ounces white button or shiitake mushrooms, sliced
1 tablespoon flour
1 teaspoon lemon juice
4 tablespoons heavy cream
Salt and pepper to taste
Sourdough bread, cut on the diagonal and toasted
Chopped parsley

TO MAKE POINTS:

◆ Melt 2 tablespoons butter in skillet over low heat; cook mushrooms until well-colored.
◆ Add remaining 2 tablespoons butter to skillet; let melt.
◆ Add flour to melted butter; stir until thickened.
◆ Add lemon juice and heavy cream slowly, stirring constantly; salt and pepper to taste.
◆ Serve over toasted bread.
◆ Top with chopped parsley.

Oysters in Williamsburg Wheat Ale™

Serves 4
Preparation time: 30 minutes
Cooking time: 10 minutes

Brewer's Pairing Suggestions:
Enjoy with a pint of
Williamsburg Brewery Wheat Ale™.
If you're leaning toward a wine, try a
dry, light white Sauvignon Blanc,
a light red like a Pinot Noir or
a Beaujolais Nouveau. Your pairing
doesn't need to be "correct."
It just needs to taste good together.
Enjoy the robust version with a
Williamsburg Porter™ or
a Cabernet Sauvignon.

24 fresh Bay or Atlantic oysters
2 tablespoons butter or rendered bacon fat
1 shallot or ½ small yellow onion, chopped fine
1 sprig fresh thyme
1 bay leaf
1 cup Williamsburg Brewery Wheat Ale™
Pinch salt
Ground black pepper
4 sprigs fresh parsley leaves, chopped coarse

TO MAKE OYSTERS:

◆ Rinse and shuck oysters.
◆ Reserve oyster liquor and the deep half of the oyster shells.
◆ Rinse deep half of oyster shells.
◆ Arrange six of the empty oyster shells on each serving plate or shallow bowl.
◆ Heat butter or bacon fat in a heavy skillet over medium-high heat.
◆ Stir in shallots, thyme and bay leaf and cook until tender, approximately one to two minutes.
◆ Stir in reserved oyster liquor, Williamsburg Brewery Wheat Ale™, salt, and pepper; heat on medium until liquid begins to bubble.
◆ Stir in oysters and heat through until edges of oysters begin to curl and liquid just starts to bubble again, approximately two to three minutes.
◆ Place one oyster in each shell; spoon some steaming liquid over all.
◆ Garnish with chopped parsley.

◆ VARIATION: *For a more robust dish prepare as above and complete recipe as follows:*

4 slices thick-cut Surry bacon
4 ounces grated Swiss cheese
½ cup dried bread crumbs

◆ Cook bacon until brown; cut each strip into six pieces.
◆ Arrange deep half of shells on a baking pan; add bacon, an oyster, a good pinch of Swiss cheese, and a pinch of bread crumbs.
◆ Heat under broiler one to two minutes until bread crumbs start to brown.
◆ Arrange on plate and serve.

The Chamberlain was a destination of choice for steamboat travelers from Baltimore. When the original Chamberlain Hotel burned down in 1920, the present edifice was erected. Today, much of the hotel has been restored to its original grandeur, with an impressive lobby and dining room.

If the view and the hotel museum are not enough to peak your interest, perhaps the legend that the hotel is haunted will attract your attention. More than one apparition, including George Washington, is said to walk the halls of this cavernous establishment.

Southern Shrimp Cakes

Advance preparation required.

Serves 8
Preparation time: 30 minutes
Cooking time: 20 minutes

Create larger cakes and serve as an entrée.

SHRIMP CAKES
- ⅛ cup cashews, finely chopped
- ¼ cup fresh bread crumbs
- ¼ pound cooked shrimp, finely chopped
- ¼ pound fresh crabmeat
- 4 ounces potato chips, finely crushed and divided
- 1 egg, beaten
- Zest of one orange
- 2 tablespoons chopped chives
- ½ cup flour
- 2 tablespoons olive oil

SAUCE
- 1 orange, juiced
- ⅛ cup balsamic vinegar or ¼ cup orange juice
- 1 tablespoon Dijon-style mustard
- ¾ cup olive oil

TO MAKE SHRIMP CAKES:
- ◆ Mix cashews, bread crumbs, shrimp, crabmeat, ⅓ cup crushed potato chips, egg, orange zest, chives, and flour.
- ◆ Refrigerate for several hours.
- ◆ Shape chilled shrimp mixture into small cakes approximately 2 inches in diameter.
- ◆ Place remaining potato chips on a plate; coat shrimp cakes with chips.
- ◆ Place shrimp cakes on wax paper and return to refrigerator for several hours to chill.
- ◆ Heat olive oil in a cast iron skillet over medium heat.
- ◆ Place three to four shrimp cakes in the hot skillet and sear for two minutes per side.
- ◆ At this point, the cakes can be served.
- ◆ Wrap cakes in foil and refrigerate.
- ◆ Reheat in preheated 350 degree oven for 20 minutes.
- ◆ Serve with a remoulade or sauce.

TO MAKE SAUCE:
- ◆ Mix orange juice, balsamic vinegar, and Dijon-style mustard in a food processor or blender.
- ◆ Slowly add olive oil; process until smooth.

from Mobjack Bay Beer Company:
Spicy Chicken Bites with Apricot Pale Ale Mustard

Advance preparation required.

Serves **8–10**
Preparation time: 30 minutes
Cooking time: 10 minutes

2 teaspoons cayenne pepper
2 teaspoons freshly ground black pepper
1 teaspoon ground white pepper
2 teaspoons ground dried thyme
1 tablespoon garlic powder
1 teaspoon salt
5 chicken breast halves, boned, skinned and cut into bite-size pieces
1½ cups apricot preserves
5 tablespoons Mobjack Bay Pale Ale
5 tablespoons creole or Dijon-style mustard
2 tablespoons butter
2 tablespoons vegetable oil

TO MAKE CHICKEN BITES:

◆ Mix cayenne pepper, black pepper, white pepper, thyme, garlic powder, and salt in bowl or plastic bag.
◆ Sprinkle chicken with spice mix.
◆ Let stand for 30 minutes.
◆ Mix apricot preserves, Mobjack Bay Pale Ale, and Dijon-style mustard in small saucepan.
◆ Heat preserve mixture over low heat until preserves melt and mixture is thoroughly blended.
◆ Set aside to cool.
◆ Heat butter and oil in skillet over medium-high heat.
◆ Add chicken and cook until just done, approximately five minutes.
◆ Remove chicken with slotted spoon and drain briefly on paper towel.
◆ Serve hot with mustard.

The Williamsburg Winery's Marinated Smithfield Ham

Advance preparation required.

Serves **4**
Preparation time: 10 minutes

Pair this recipe with The Williamsburg Winery Burgesses Measure Merlot

¼ pound country cured Smithfield ham, thinly sliced
¼ teaspoon black pepper
1 tablespoon Virginia vodka
1 tablespoon fresh lemon juice
1 teaspoon finely chopped fresh dill

TO MAKE HAM:

◆ Place bite-size pieces of country cured Smithfield ham on a serving plate.
◆ Sprinkle with black pepper, vodka, lemon juice, and dill.
◆ Cover and refrigerate for several hours.
◆ Serve cold with toothpicks or on a water cracker.

Fresh lemon juice is a necessity for this recipe's success.

Ingleside's Blue Crab Red Mulled Wine

Serves **10**
Preparation time: 5 minutes
Cooking time: 30 minutes

A warm treat for a cool evening.

Cheesecloth
5 whole cloves
1 bottle (750 ml) Ingleside Plantation Vineyards Blue Crab Red Wine
1 quart apple juice
3 limes, sliced
3 lemons, sliced
4 oranges, sliced
1 cup brown sugar
1 teaspoon allspice

TO MAKE MULLED WINE:

- Cut a square of cheesecloth; place cloves in the middle of cheesecloth.
- Bring ends of cheesecloth together and tie with string to close.
- Pour wine into a large pot.
- Add cloves, apple juice, limes, lemons, oranges, brown sugar, and all spice; simmer for 30 minutes.
- Remove whole cloves in cheesecloth bag.
- Serve warm.

Hot Spiked Cider

Advance preparation required.

Serves **16**
Preparation time: 20 minutes
Cooking time: 20 minutes

You can keep this warm in a crock pot for several hours.

2 quarts apple cider
1 cup dried apricot halves
1 cup golden raisins
1 cup dried apple slices
¾ cup peach or ginger flavored brandy
2 whole cloves, wrapped in cheesecloth for easy removal
½ teaspoon ground ginger
¼ teaspoon ground cinnamon
1 cup bourbon
Cinnamon sticks

TO MAKE CIDER:

- Mix apple cider, apricot halves, golden raisins, apple slices, brandy, whole cloves, and ground cinnamon in a large stainless saucepan.
- Let stand at room temperature for at least one hour.
- Heat cider mixture over medium heat until hot.
- Remove from heat; discard cloves.
- Stir in bourbon.
- Garnish with cinnamon sticks.
- Serve hot.

Blue Suede Smooth

Serves 2
Preparation time: 5 minutes

Even Elvis would have liked this...

2 cups frozen blueberries
8 ounces vanilla yogurt
1 cup milk
4 tablespoons maple syrup
1 teaspoon cinnamon

TO MAKE BEVERAGE:

◆ Place all ingredients in blender; process until smooth.
◆ Serve immediately.

---

from Ingleside Plantation Vineyards:
Northern Neck Sangria

Serves 6
Preparation time: 5 minutes

A cool southern blend to quench your summer's thirst.

1 bottle (750 ml) Ingleside Colonial Rose wine, chilled
2 liters Northern Neck Ginger Ale™, chilled
16 ounces mixed frozen fruit
Vanilla ice cream

TO MAKE BEVERAGE:

◆ Mix chilled wine and ginger ale in a large punch bowl.
◆ Stir in frozen fruit; mix well.
◆ Add a scoop of vanilla ice cream to each glass for a special treat.

Lee's Traveler

Serves 1
Preparation time: 5 minutes

A crisp and refreshing beverage from Alpenglow Sparkling Cider; use for any occasion when a mimosa or wine spritzer is appropriate.

1½ ounces Bowman's™ Virginia Vodka
1 beverage glass, 6-ounce size
Crushed ice
Alpenglow Sparkling Cider
Slice of apple

TO MAKE BEVERAGE:

◆ Pour vodka into beverage glass.
◆ Stir in crushed ice.
◆ Fill with Alpenglow Sparkling Cider.
◆ Garnish with a slice of apple.
◆ Enjoy!

Love and Kisses Menu

(Engagements, weddings, anniversaries)

◆

The Williamsburg Winery's Marinated Smithfield Ham
Pair with The Williamsburg Winery Burgesses' Measure Merlot

◆

Brie Strata with Pungo Salsa

Hunt Country Cheese Grits

Marinated Asparagus

Mixed Greens dressed with Celebration Dressing

Pair with Loudoun Valley Vineyards Vinifera White

◆

Pretty and Pink Marble Pound Cake served

with fresh strawberries and whipped cream

Pair with La Provencale Cellars Le Mousseux Sparkling Virginia Cider

*Here's to your past
for all that you have been.
Here's to your present
for all that you are.
Here's to your future
for all that you will be.*

—Toast written by Tracie Pruden, JLNVB member

Brie Strata with Pungo Salsa

Advance preparation required.

Serves 6
Preparation time: 20 minutes
Cooking time: 35–40 minutes

Pair this recipe with Loudoun Valley Vineyards Vinifera White.

A great time to make this recipe is during the Pungo Strawberry Festival.

BRIE STRATA
10 slices white bread, ½ inch thick (sourdough, challah, etc.)
3 tablespoons butter, softened
16 ounces Brie cheese, rind removed and cubed
10 ounces fresh spinach, stems removed
4 eggs, beaten
2 cups milk
1 teaspoon chervil
1 teaspoon salt

PUNGO SALSA
1 pint fresh strawberries, stems removed
1 large pear, peeled
1 tablespoon honey
1 tablespoon lime juice
1 tablespoon candied ginger, finely chopped

TO MAKE STRATA:
- Butter one side of each slice of bread.
- Cut bread into bite-size cubes.
- Grease a 9 X 9 inch baking pan.
- Line the bottom of pan with half of the bread, butter side up.
- Place half of the cubed Brie cheese on top of bread cubes.
- Steam spinach in a small amount of water.
- Squeeze excess water out of spinach.
- Spread spinach on top of Brie cheese.
- Top Brie cheese with remaining half of the bread cubes.
- Top bread cubes with the remaining half of the Brie cheese.
- Stir eggs and milk together; mix well.
- Add chervil and salt to egg mixture; mix well.
- Pour egg mixture over bread and cheese.
- Let the strata stand for at least 30 minutes or cover and refrigerate overnight.
- Bring back to room temperature before baking if refrigerated.
- Bake in preheated 350 degree oven for 35–40 minutes.
- Let stand for 10 minutes before cutting and serving with Pungo Salsa.

TO MAKE PUNGO SALSA:
- Dice strawberries and pear.
- Pour honey and lime juice over strawberries and pear; sprinkle with candied ginger.
- Toss to combine.
- Place salsa on top of cut strata.

Overnight Fruited French Toast

Advance preparation required.

Serves 6
Preparation time: 15 minutes
Cooking time: 20–25 minutes

**Pair this recipe with
Oasis Winery Brut.**

1 loaf raisin pecan bread
5 eggs
¾ cup milk
¼ teaspoon baking powder
1 tablespoon vanilla extract
20 ounces frozen whole strawberries
4 ripe bananas, sliced
½ cup sugar
1½ tablespoons cinnamon, divided
1 tablespoon sugar

TO MAKE FRENCH TOAST:

◆ Grease 8 X 8 baking pan.
◆ Cut bread into six or more thick slices.
◆ Place bread in prepared baking pan.
◆ Mix together eggs, milk, baking powder, and vanilla extract.
◆ Pour egg mixture over bread, cover, and refrigerate.
◆ Turn bread over after an hour to make sure the egg mixture soaks in evenly.
◆ Re-cover and refrigerate overnight.
◆ Preheat oven to 450 degrees when ready to bake.
◆ Mix strawberries, bananas, sugar, and ½ tablespoon cinnamon.
◆ Remove bread from pan and place fruit mixture on bottom of pan.
◆ Place bread back on top of fruit mixture.
◆ Mix 1 tablespoon sugar and remaining cinnamon; sprinkle on top of bread.
◆ Bake in 450 degree oven for 20–25 minutes.

Virginia Harvest Quiche

Advance preparation required.

Serves **12**
Preparation time: 45 minutes
Cooking time: 2 hours

Pair this recipe with La Provencale Cellars Le Mousseux Sparkling Virginia Cider or The Williamsburg Winery Governor's White.

This recipe is a nice surprise!

PASTRY
2 cups flour
1 teaspoon salt
¼ teaspoon sugar
12 tablespoons cold butter, cut into small pieces
1 egg yolk, beaten
3 tablespoons ice water

FILLING
4 cups half-and-half
4 eggs, beaten
¼ teaspoon kosher salt
¼ teaspoon pepper
⅛ teaspoon nutmeg
2 tablespoons butter
1¼ pounds Virginia ham, chopped
1 pound Granny Smith apples, peeled, thinly sliced and cut into matchstick size
¼ teaspoon cinnamon
8 ounces sharp Cheddar cheese, shredded
½ cup toasted peanuts, chopped

TO MAKE PASTRY:
- Mix flour, salt, and sugar in a bowl.
- Mix butter into flour with a pastry blender until the mixture looks like coarse crumbs.
- Mix egg yolk and ice water; add to the pastry mixture.
- Mix until the dough comes together and binds. It should not be sticky or overly dry.
- Form dough into a ball and wrap in plastic wrap; refrigerate for at least 30 minutes.
- Sprinkle flour over rolling surface and rolling pin.
- Remove dough, place on floured surface, and roll out into a 14-inch circle.
- Spray bottom of 9-inch springform pan with nonstick cooking spray.
- Transfer and mold dough into springform pan; return pan to the refrigerator for 30 minutes.

TO MAKE FILLING:
- Whisk half-and-half, eggs, kosher salt, pepper, and nutmeg in a bowl; set aside.
- Melt butter in a skillet over medium-low heat; mix in ham and apples.
- Cook for three to four minutes.
- Preheat oven to 350 degrees.
- Sprinkle cinnamon over ham and apples; mix thoroughly.

Continued on next page...

continued from page 28:

TO MAKE FILLING:

- Remove ham and apples from skillet with a slotted spoon; place in pastry shell.
- Cover ham and apples with Cheddar cheese.
- Pour milk mixture over Cheddar cheese.
- Sprinkle toasted peanuts over cheese.
- Cover top of quiche with aluminum foil.
- Place in a preheated 350 degree oven for 1 hour and 30 minutes.
- Remove aluminum foil and continue baking for an additional 30 minutes or until the quiche is set.

Fresh Tomato & Zucchini Tart

Serves 6
Preparation time: 25 minutes
Cooking time: 20–25 minutes

Pair this recipe with Prince Michel & Rapidan River Vineyards Madison Reserve Rose or Breaux Vineyards Sauvignon Blanc.

This is a perfect way to use the abundance of zucchini available in the summer.

1 (9-inch) refrigerated pie crust
5 ounces Gruyére cheese, shredded and divided
4 ounces Parmesan cheese, shredded and divided
Fresh chopped basil
4–5 plum tomatoes, thinly sliced rounds
3 zucchini, thinly sliced rounds
Sea salt
Olive oil

TO MAKE TART:

- Preheat oven to 425 degrees.
- Spray tart pan with nonstick cooking spray.
- Place pie crust in tart pan.
- Fit crust to the edges of tart pan.
- Spread half of the Gruyére and Parmesan cheeses on bottom of crust.
- Sprinkle basil over cheeses to taste.
- Sprinkle tomatoes and zucchini with sea salt; drain on paper towel for five minutes.
- Layer tomatoes and zucchini alternately in an overlapping pattern on top of cheeses and basil starting at the outer edge of the crust.
- Spread remaining Gruyére and Parmesan cheese over tomatoes and zucchini.
- Start in the opposite direction for the second layer of tomatoes and zucchini.
- Fill in tart completely.
- Drizzle with olive oil.
- Bake in preheated 425 degree oven for 20–25 minutes.
- Remove from oven, dust with additional Parmesan cheese, and serve immediately.

Ham & Goat Cheese Strata

Advance preparation required.

Serves **6**
Preparation time: 30 minutes
Cooking time: 55 minutes

**Pair this recipe with
Linden Vineyards Seyval.**

Goat cheese adds a different flavor
to this long-time favorite.

12 slices white bread, crusts removed
12 ounces goat cheese, crumbled
2 cups diced ham or 1 pound sausage, cooked and drained
½ cup minced onions
6 eggs, lightly beaten
3½ cups milk
½ teaspoon salt
1 teaspoon Dijon-style mustard
¼ teaspoon nutmeg

TO MAKE STRATA:

◆ Lightly butter or coat with nonstick cooking spray a 13 X 9 X 2 inch baking dish or large shallow baking dish.
◆ Cut one circle from center of each bread slice with a biscuit cutter and set aside.
◆ Place remaining bread scraps on bottom of prepared baking dish.
◆ Layer goat cheese and meat over top of bread; sprinkle with onion.
◆ Arrange bread circles over top of goat cheese and meat.
◆ Mix milk, salt, Dijon-style mustard, and nutmeg into beaten eggs.
◆ Pour egg mixture over bread and cheese.
◆ Cover dish with plastic wrap; refrigerate overnight or for up to 24 hours.
◆ Bring strata to room temperature before baking.
◆ Uncover strata; bake in preheated 325 degree oven for 55 minutes.
◆ Let stand for 10 minutes before cutting and serving.

Hunt Country Cheese Grits

Serves 8
Preparation time: 20 minutes
Cooking time: 60 minutes

Pair this recipe with Loudoun Valley Vineyards Vinifera White.

Typical of an Old Virginia
Hunt Country brunch.

1 quart milk
8 tablespoons butter
1 cup quick-cooking grits
5⅓ tablespoons butter
1 teaspoon salt
½ teaspoon pepper
4 ounces Gruyére cheese, chopped
1 cup raw oysters, drained
1 ounce Parmesan cheese, shredded

TO MAKE GRITS:

◆ Preheat oven to 350 degrees.
◆ Grease a 3-quart baking dish.
◆ Bring milk to a boil in a medium saucepan over medium heat.
◆ Mix in 8 tablespoons butter; let melt.
◆ Mix in grits, stirring until thickened, approximately five to seven minutes.
◆ Stir in 5⅓ tablespoons butter to grits; let butter melt.
◆ Reduce heat to low.
◆ Stir salt and pepper into grits mixture.
◆ Stir Gruyére cheese and oysters into grits mixture; mix well.
◆ Pour grits mixture into a prepared baking dish.
◆ Sprinkle with Parmesan cheese.
◆ Bake in preheated 350 degree oven for 60 minutes.
◆ Let stand for 10 minutes before serving.

FOR A FANCIER PRESENTATION:

◆ Evenly divide grits and place in greased ramekins.
◆ Sprinkle with fresh bread crumbs.
◆ Bake for 40 minutes.

Chile Egg Frittata

Serves 10–12
Preparation time: 15 minutes
Cooking time: 35 minutes

**Pair this recipe with
Rockbridge Vineyard White Riesling.**

Everybody's favorite—
a must-make brunch entrée.

10 eggs
½ cup flour
1 teaspoon baking powder
½ teaspoon salt
1 teaspoon cumin
16 ounces small curd cottage cheese
16 ounces Monterey Jack cheese, shredded
8 tablespoons butter, melted
8 ounces diced green chilies

TO MAKE FRITTATA:

◆ Preheat oven to 350 degrees if baking immediately.
◆ Butter 13 X 9 X 2 baking dish.
◆ Beat eggs thoroughly with an electric mixer in a large bowl.
◆ Mix in flour, baking powder, salt, cumin, cottage cheese, Monterey Jack cheese, and butter.
◆ Stir green chilies into the egg mixture.
◆ Pour mixture into prepared 13 X 9 X 2 baking dish.
◆ The frittata can be assembled the night before, refrigerated, and baked later.
◆ Bring frittata to room temperature before baking.
◆ Bake in preheated 350 degrees oven for 35 minutes or until top is browned and center appears firm.
◆ Serve hot.

Poached Eggs on a Bed of Veggies

Serves 4
Preparation time: 20 minutes
Cooking time: 10–15 minutes

**Pair this recipe with First Colony Winery
Vidal Blanc or Barboursville Vineyards Brut.**

Dill-icious eggs.

3 tablespoons butter
1 cup chopped onions
2 cups sliced mushrooms
1 cup sliced red and green bell peppers
Fresh chopped garlic to taste
Salt and pepper to taste
Dash of cayenne pepper
2 tablespoons fresh dill, minced
1 tomato, chopped
¼ cup sour cream
4 eggs

TO MAKE POACHED EGGS:

◆ Melt butter in a large skillet; add onions, mushrooms, and bell peppers; cook until tender.
◆ Add garlic, salt, pepper, cayenne, dill, tomato, and sour cream; stir until well blended.
◆ Break eggs over tops of vegetables.
◆ Cover pan; poach eggs over medium heat until set, approximately 3–5 minutes.

Sweet Basil Scones

Serves **8**
Preparation time: 30 minutes
Cooking time: 10–13 minutes

2½ cups flour
1 tablespoon baking powder
1 teaspoon salt
1½ tablespoons chopped fresh sweet basil
1½ teaspoons baking soda
4 tablespoons butter
1 roma tomato, seeded and finely chopped
½ cup milk
¼ cup honey, warmed
1 tablespoon water
1 egg yolk
2 teaspoons sugar

TO MAKE SCONES:

◆ Preheat oven to 400 degrees.
◆ Mix flour, baking powder, salt, basil, and baking soda.
◆ Cut butter into flour mixture until it resembles coarse meal.
◆ Add chopped tomato to flour mixture.
◆ Mix milk, warmed honey, and water in a small bowl until honey dissolves.
◆ Pour milk mixture into flour mixture; stir until soft dough forms.
◆ Form a dough ball and sprinkle outside of dough ball with flour.
◆ Spread dough onto a lightly floured surface.
◆ Roll dough out to approximately ¾ to 1 inch thick.
◆ Cut dough with a 3-inch biscuit cutter; place on a nonstick cookie sheet.
◆ Brush tops of dough with egg yolk; sprinkle with remaining sugar.
◆ Bake in preheated 400 degree oven for 10–13 minutes or until golden brown.

Orange Pecan Biscotti

Advance preparation required.

Yields 20 cookies
Preparation time: 30 minutes
Cooking time: 55 minutes

4 eggs
1 cup sugar
1½ tablespoons grated orange rind
2 tablespoons vegetable oil
1 teaspoon vanilla extract
1 teaspoon almond extract
3⅓ cups flour
2 teaspoons baking powder
1 cup chopped pecans

TO MAKE BISCOTTI:

◆ Beat eggs and sugar with a mixer at high speed for five minutes.
◆ Mix in orange rind, vegetable oil, vanilla extract, and almond extract.
◆ Beat until blended.
◆ Mix flour and baking powder in a separate bowl.
◆ Mix flour mixture into the egg and sugar mixture, beating well.
◆ Fold pecans into dough.
◆ Cover dough and freeze for 30 minutes or until firm.
◆ Preheat oven to 325 degrees.
◆ Divide dough in half.
◆ Shape each portion into an 8 X 5 inch log.
◆ Place log on a cookie sheet lined with parchment paper.
◆ Bake in preheated 325 degree oven for 25 minutes or until firm.
◆ Cool on baking sheet for five minutes.
◆ Remove to wire racks to cool completely.
◆ Cut each log diagonally into ½-inch-thick slices with a serrated knife.
◆ Place slices on greased baking sheets.
◆ Bake in 325 degree oven for 15 minutes.
◆ Turn biscotti over and bake for an additional 15 minutes.
◆ Remove to wire racks and cool.

No Bother Rolls

Advance preparation required.

Yields **24** rolls
Preparation time: 20 minutes
Cooking time: 20–25 minutes

Even if you're not a bread maker, try these delicious rolls.

2 packages (¼ ounce each) active dry yeast
½ cup lukewarm water
16 ounces cottage cheese
½ cup sugar
2 teaspoons salt
½ teaspoon baking soda
2 eggs, slightly beaten
4½ cups sifted flour

TO MAKE ROLLS:

◆ Dissolve yeast in lukewarm water.

◆ Heat cottage cheese until lukewarm, approximately 95 degrees.

◆ Mix lukewarm cottage cheese, sugar, salt, baking soda, eggs, and yeast mixture in large bowl.

◆ Add flour gradually to the cottage cheese mixture, mixing well after each addition.

◆ Place dough into greased bowl; cover with plastic wrap.

◆ Let dough rise until double, approximately 90 minutes.

◆ Punch dough down; turn onto lightly floured surface.

◆ Divide dough into 24 equal pieces.

◆ Place dough pieces into well-greased 13 X 9 X 2 pan.

◆ Cover with a clean tea towel; let dough rise for an additional hour.

◆ Preheat oven to 350 degrees.

◆ Bake in preheated 350 degree oven for 20–25 minutes or until golden brown.

Southern Batter Bread

Serves **6**
Preparation time: 15 minutes
Cooking time: 20–25 minutes

A cast iron skillet is a necessity for this old Virginia recipe updated for today's diet.

1 teaspoon grapeseed oil
1 cup stone ground cornmeal
1 cup boiling water
1 cup buttermilk
2 eggs
1 tablespoon grapeseed oil
1 teaspoon baking soda

TO MAKE BREAD:

◆ Preheat oven to 450 degrees.
◆ Pour 1 teaspoon grapeseed oil into 9- or 10-inch, well-seasoned cast iron skillet.
◆ Make sure the skillet is completely coated with the grapeseed oil.
◆ Heat skillet over medium heat until hot, approximately five minutes.
◆ Mix cornmeal and boiling water in a bowl; mix thoroughly.
◆ Mix the buttermilk, eggs, 1 tablespoon grapeseed oil, and baking soda into the corn meal mixture; mix thoroughly.
◆ Pour batter into hot skillet.
◆ Bake in preheated 450 degree oven for 20–25 minutes or until top is golden brown.
◆ Turn baked bread out of skillet onto a warm platter.

New Additions Menu

(Births, Adoptions, and Christenings)

◆

Elegant Pesto Torte

Spicy Chicken Bites with Apricot Pale Ale Mustard

Pair with Linden Vineyards Riesling Vidal or

Farfelu Vineyards Fou de Rouge

◆

Virginia Bouillabaisse from The Williamsburg Winery

Southern Batter Bread

Pair with The Williamsburg Winery's Acte 12 Chardonnay

◆

Pecan Pie with Kahlua® and Chocolate Chips

Enjoy with coffee

Section photograph dedicated to:
JLNVB Community Partners

*Here's to the joy, wonder,
and amazement of new life
and all that it will hold!*

—*Toast written by Tracie Pruden, JLNVB member*

Water, water everywhere. That's what brought the first settlers in the 1600s to Poquoson. An Indian word for "great marsh," Poquoson is considered to be one of the older English-speaking communities in America that has retained its original name. This one-time fishing village is located at the mouth of the Chesapeake Bay between the Poquoson River, Back River, and Wythe Creek.

As early as 1635, Poquoson's waterways were used to ship the Tidewater area's major cash crop, tobacco, to neighboring and distant ports. Eventually, Poquoson's aquatic avenues became a launching point for one of its leading industries—seafood. The seafood business still has a strong hold on the town's economy today.

from Rebec Vineyards:

Spiced Black Bean Soup with Garlic Puree

Serves 6
Preparation time: 40 minutes
Cooking time: 2 hours

This recipe was the
1992 Virginia Garlic Festival Winner
held at Rebec Vineyards.

GARLIC PUREE
8 cloves elephant garlic
2½ cups water
4 tablespoons butter

SOUP
3 tablespoons olive oil
1 large onion, chopped
3 cloves garlic, crushed and minced
1 teaspoon garlic powder
1 teaspoon celery seed
1½ teaspoons minced fresh thyme
1½ teaspoons minced fresh sage
4 teaspoons ground cumin
2 teaspoons coriander
¼ teaspoon cayenne pepper
3 bay leaves
2 beef bouillon cubes
3¾ cups cooked black beans
½ cup dry red Virginia wine
1 can (28 ounces) chopped tomatoes, undrained
1 pound kielbasa, cut into ⅛-inch slices
2 tablespoons chopped fresh parsley

TO MAKE GARLIC PUREE:
◆ Peel garlic cloves; cut into quarters.
◆ Place cut garlic in a heavy bottomed pan and add water and butter.
◆ Cook over low heat, stirring occasionally until garlic is soft and can be mashed with a spoon.
◆ This may take a while and you may need to add more water before garlic is soft.
◆ Drain water when garlic is cooked.
◆ Transfer garlic to a food processor fitted with a steel blade and puree.
◆ Set pureed garlic aside and refrigerate until ready to use.

TO MAKE SOUP:
◆ Heat olive oil in a large pot over medium-low heat; add onion, garlic, garlic powder, celery seed, thyme, sage, cumin, coriander, and cayenne pepper.
◆ Cook mixture, stirring frequently for 10 minutes.
◆ Stir in bay leaves, bouillon cubes, black beans, red wine, and tomatoes.
◆ Cook over medium-low heat for 60 minutes, stirring frequently.
◆ Add kielbasa and cook over medium low heat for an additional 60 minutes or until thickened, stirring frequently to keep from sticking to the bottom of the pan.

Continued on next page...

continued from page 40:

TO MAKE SOUP:

- Remove bay leaves before serving.
- Ladle soup into bowls and spoon a tablespoon of the garlic puree on top of each portion.
- Sprinkle with fresh parsley.

from The Williamsburg Winery:

Virginia Bouillabaisse

Serves 6
Preparation time: 45 minutes
Cooking time: 55 minutes

**Pair this recipe with
The Williamsburg Winery
Acte 12 Chardonnay.**

Virginia seafood at its finest. For added presentation, steam clams and mussels in their shells and keep in shells when placing in bowls.

1 pound (36 count) shrimp with shells
5 cups water
1 cup Williamsburg Winery Chardonnay
1 pound roma tomatoes, deseeded, pulp removed and chopped
1 cup fresh clams, shucked (approximately 3 dozen)
2 cups fresh mussels, shucked (approximately 2 dozen)
1 teaspoon fresh thyme
1 teaspoon kosher salt
1 teaspoon fresh parsley
1 teaspoon saffron or 1 teaspoon Sazón Goya® con azafrán
1 teaspoon black pepper
2 teaspoons minced garlic
1 teaspoon fresh oregano
1 tablespoon olive oil
8 ounces fresh crabmeat
1 green bell pepper, chopped
1 yellow bell pepper, chopped

TO MAKE BOUILLABAISE:

- Peel the shrimp; place shrimp shells in 2-quart pot.
- Pour water and Williamsburg Winery Chardonnay over shrimp shells; bring to a boil.
- Reduce heat; simmer for 30 minutes.
- Strain broth, removing shrimp shells.
- Place chopped tomatoes in 3-quart pot.
- Pour broth over tomatoes.
- Add clams, mussels, thyme, kosher salt, parsley, saffron, pepper, garlic, oregano, and olive oil; simmer over low heat for 12 minutes.
- Add crabmeat and simmer for an additional 12 minutes.
- Grill or cook the shrimp.
- Divide bell peppers evenly between six soup bowls.
- Pour soup over vegetables; top with cooked shrimp.
- Serve with crusty garlic or sourdough bread.

While Virginia Beach is best known as a resort area and the most populous city in Virginia, it can also claim a piece of American history.

Before the first permanent English settlers traveled up the James River to found Jamestown, they stopped at Cape Henry, a spot where the Atlantic Ocean meets the Chesapeake Bay. On April 26, 1607, three ships—the Susan Constant, Godspeed, and Discovery—anchored in the Chesapeake Bay just off what is now Cape Henry. Captain George Percy led a landing party ashore where they found tall trees and fresh waters running through the woods. They named the area after King James' son, Henry Prince of Wales.

Today, the nearby Cape Henry lighthouse—built after the American Revolution—and a cross erected in 1935 remind us of this historic landing.

Nouveau Chili

Serves **10**
Preparation time: 45 minutes
Cooking time: 45 minutes

Pair this recipe with Oakencroft Vineyard & Winery Countryside Red.

If you like spicy dishes, this one is for you. You can add beans for a heartier meal.

1 tablespoon butter
2 medium red or Vidalia onions, chopped
1½ pounds mushrooms, sliced
3 pounds lean ground beef
12 plum tomatoes
3 cans (6 ounces each) roasted garlic tomato paste
16 ounces hot cherry peppers, seeded, chopped, and juice saved
12 ounces St. George Pilsner
2–3 tablespoons chili powder
1 tablespoon cumin
Tortilla chips
Shredded Cheddar cheese
Sour cream

TO MAKE CHILI:

◆ Melt butter in a large pot over medium-low heat; stir in onions and mushrooms.
◆ Cook until tender, approximately 10 minutes.
◆ Add ground beef and cook until done.
◆ Cut plum tomatoes in half; remove seeds and pulp; chop plum tomatoes.
◆ Stir plum tomatoes and tomato paste into ground beef mixture; mix thoroughly.
◆ Add cherry peppers with juice, St. George Pilsner, chili powder, and cumin; mix thoroughly.
◆ Simmer for at least 15 minutes.
◆ Serve with tortilla chips.
◆ Garnish with shredded Cheddar cheese and sour cream.

from Lake Anna Winery:

Roquefort Vichyssoise

Serves 12
Preparation time: 35 minutes
Cooking time: 40 minutes

Pair this recipe with Lake Anna Winery Chardonnay.

This is great served hot or cold.

6 tablespoons butter
4 large onions, thinly sliced
1 teaspoon minced garlic
6 medium all-purpose potatoes, peeled and cut in 1-inch chunks,
   approximately 3 pounds
3 cups chicken stock or canned low-sodium broth, or more if necessary
1 cup Lake Anna Winery Chardonnay
2 cups light cream
⅔ cup heavy cream
8 ounces crumbled Roquefort cheese, divided
Salt and freshly ground pepper

TO MAKE SOUP:

◆ Melt butter in a large, heavy, non-reactive saucepan over medium-high heat.
◆ Stir in onions and garlic; cook until the onions are soft but not brown.
◆ Stir in potatoes, stirring to coat with butter; cook for five minutes.
◆ Stir in chicken stock and Lake Anna Winery Chardonnay; bring to a boil.
◆ Reduce heat to low; cover and simmer until the potatoes are tender, approximately 30 minutes.
◆ Let cool.
◆ Stir in light and heavy cream and gently reheat the soup; do not boil.
◆ Stir in half of Roquefort cheese.
◆ Transfer the soup to a blender and puree in small batches until smooth.
◆ Season with salt and pepper to taste.
◆ Thin with additional stock or wine, if necessary.
◆ Garnish with the remaining crumbled Roquefort cheese.

Velvety Sweet Potato Soup

Serves **6**
Preparation time: 25 minutes
Cooking time: 60 minutes

Pair this recipe with Jefferson Vineyards Merlot.

A wonderful addition to your family's Thanksgiving dinner.

SOUP
- $1\frac{1}{2}$ tablespoons butter
- 1 small onion, chopped
- 5 cups chicken stock
- 2 pounds sweet potatoes, peeled and cubed
- 2 tablespoons real maple syrup
- $\frac{1}{2}$ teaspoon dried thyme
- $\frac{1}{2}$ teaspoon curry powder
- $\frac{1}{2}$ cup heavy cream
- $\frac{1}{4}$ teaspoon salt
- $\frac{1}{8}$ teaspoon pepper
- Pinch of fresh ground nutmeg
- Pinch of ground red pepper

RUM CREAM SAUCE
- $\frac{1}{2}$ cup heavy cream
- $\frac{1}{8}$ teaspoon grated lemon rind
- $\frac{1}{4}$ teaspoon fresh lemon juice
- $1\frac{1}{2}$ tablespoons dark rum

TO MAKE SOUP:
- ◆ Melt butter in a large pan over medium-high heat; stir in onion and cook until tender.
- ◆ Stir in chicken stock, sweet potatoes, maple syrup, thyme, and curry powder; bring to a boil.
- ◆ Reduce heat and simmer about 60 minutes or until sweet potato is tender.
- ◆ Cool slightly; process mixture in small batches in a blender until smooth.
- ◆ Return pureed mixture to pan; stir in heavy cream, salt, pepper, ground nutmeg, and red pepper.
- ◆ Cook over low heat, stirring occasionally until thoroughly heated.
- ◆ Serve with rum cream sauce.

TO MAKE RUM SAUCE:
- ◆ Beat heavy cream, lemon rind, lemon juice, and rum at high speed with electric mixer until soft peaks form.
- ◆ Serve on hot soup.

Williamsburg Pale Ale™ & Cheddar Soup

Serves 4
Preparation time: 25 minutes
Cooking time: 20–25 minutes

**Pair this recipe with
Williamsburg Brewing Company Pale Ale™.**

Here's a perennial brewpub favorite with a little local Tidewater flavor.

4 tablespoons butter
½ cup peeled and chopped onion
¼ cup peeled and chopped carrots
¼ cup chopped celery
¼ cup flour
2 cups chicken stock
12 ounces Williamsburg Pale Ale™
8 ounces medium Cheddar cheese, shredded
Pinch salt
Pinch ground black pepper
½ cup fresh roasted Virginia peanuts, shelled and coarsely chopped
Few shakes of hot pepper sauce

TO MAKE SOUP:

- Heat butter in heavy 4-quart saucepan; stir in onions, carrots, and celery.
- Cook on medium-high heat until onions begin to soften and just begin to get translucent, approximately two minutes.
- Stir in flour and stir with whisk; cook until roux begins to bubble, approximately two minutes.
- Mix in chicken stock; whisk until smooth and bubbling.
- Stir in Williamsburg Pale Ale™ and whisk to blend.
- Mix in Cheddar cheese; stir and heat until creamy and bubbling.
- Season with salt and ground black pepper.
- Ladle into serving bowl, garnish with chopped peanuts, and add a shake or two of hot pepper sauce.

Strawberry Soup

Advance preparation required

Serves 8
Preparation time: 25 minutes
Cooking time: 15–20 minutes

Refreshing and pleasant taste makes the perfect light, spring or summer dinner.

1½ quarts fresh strawberries
5 cups cold white grape juice
1 cup dry white wine
1 tablespoon fresh lemon juice
¾ cup sugar
1 cup plain yogurt
1 cup light cream

TO MAKE SOUP:

- Puree strawberries in a food processor or blender.
- Pour pureed strawberries into a medium saucepan.
- Mix in cold white grape juice, white wine, and lemon juice; bring to a boil.
- Boil for two minutes over medium heat.
- Stir in sugar; cook for an additional six minutes.
- Cover and refrigerate for several hours or overnight.
- Stir in yogurt and light cream several hours before serving.
- Return to refrigerator to chill thoroughly before serving.

Spinach & Feta Soup

Serves 6
Preparation time: 50 minutes
Cooking time: 40 minutes

Pair this recipe with Rockbridge Vineyard Tuscarora White.

If you do not have turmeric, leave it out or substitute ground ginger.

2 tablespoons oil
2 tablespoons butter
2 cups chopped onion
2 teaspoons chopped garlic
2 cups finely chopped fresh spinach
4 tablespoons flour
4 cups milk
2 cups chicken or vegetable broth
¼ teaspoon white pepper
¼ teaspoon turmeric (or ground ginger)
8 ounces crumbled Feta cheese
2 cups chopped cooked chicken, optional
Crumbled Feta cheese for garnish

TO MAKE SOUP:

◆ Pour oil into a saucepan.
◆ Melt butter in oil over medium heat until bubbly.
◆ Stir in onions and garlic; cook three minutes or until soft.
◆ Mix in spinach; cook an additional three minutes.
◆ Reduce heat to low.
◆ Stir in flour; cook for one minute.
◆ Stir milk into spinach-flour mixture, very slowly, incorporating approximately ⅛ cup milk into spinach-flour mixture at a time before adding more milk.
◆ When all the milk has been added, stir in broth, white pepper, and turmeric.
◆ Simmer for 20 minutes, stirring occasionally.
◆ Puree mixture in blender; return pureed mixture to pot.
◆ Stir in Feta; simmer for five minutes.
◆ Stir in chicken and simmer for an additional five minutes.
◆ Serve hot.
◆ Garnish with crumbled Feta cheese.

Visitors to Portsmouth's Olde Towne district can enjoy the largest concentration of antique homes between Alexandria, Virginia, and Charleston, South Carolina. Historic homes, such as the one shared by President Cleveland's parents, are nestled among churches and monuments in this well-preserved historic district. Explore Olde Towne on a trolley tour or take a self-guided walking tour with a brochure from the Portsmouth Visitor's Information Center. On Tuesday nights during the summer months, costumed guides lead visitors through Olde Towne at twilight, sharing local folklore and providing information about the architecture of the historic buildings.

Chicken, Gorgonzola, & Pear Salad

Serves 4–6
Preparation time: 25 minutes

Pair this recipe with Oakencroft Vineyard & Winery Chardonnay.

⅓ cup extra virgin olive oil

3 tablespoons red wine vinegar

2 tablespoons honey Dijon mustard

Salt and pepper

3 cups diced cooked chicken breast

½ cup walnuts, toasted

2 ounces crumbled Gorgonzola cheese

14-16 ounces mixed salad greens

2 pears, halved, cored and sliced

Lemon juice

TO MAKE SALAD:

◆ Whisk olive oil, red wine vinegar, honey Dijon mustard, and salt and pepper to taste in a bowl to make dressing.

◆ Mix chicken, toasted walnuts, and Gorgonzola cheese; pour dressing over chicken and toss to coat ingredients with dressing.

◆ Place greens on individual salad plates.

◆ Dip pears in lemon juice to keep from turning brown.

◆ Arrange sliced pears in fan shape along one side of greens.

◆ Remove chicken from dressing with slotted spoon; arrange equally over greens.

◆ Drizzle any remaining dressing over chicken, pears, and greens.

Tangy Tomato Chutney

Yields 2½ cups
Preparation time: 20 minutes
Cooking time: 60 minutes

Need a great sandwich condiment?
Try this on a chicken sandwich
or as a topping for warm Brie cheese.

1 can (28 ounces) whole tomatoes, chopped, liquid reserved
1 large onion, chopped
Zest of 1 lemon, minced
½ cup sugar
½ cup cider vinegar
⅓ cup dried currants
1½ teaspoons mustard seeds
½ teaspoon salt
¼ teaspoon cayenne
¼ teaspoon ground allspice
¼ teaspoon cinnamon

TO MAKE CHUTNEY:

- Mix tomatoes, reserved liquid, onion, lemon zest, sugar, cider vinegar, currants, mustard seeds, salt, cayenne, allspice, and cinnamon in a heavy skillet.
- Cook mixture over moderate heat for 30 minutes; stir occasionally.
- Reduce heat to low and simmer, uncovered, for an additional 30 minutes; stir occasionally.
- Will reduce to approximately 2½ cups of chutney.
- Keeps in refrigerator for up to three months.

---

from Cooper Vineyards:
Sweet Louisa Fruit Compote

Yields 4 cups
Preparation time: 20 minutes
Cooking time: 45–60 minutes

Excellent as a sandwich condiment with
ham, roast pork, turkey or duck.
Also can be used as a topping for ice cream,
pound cake or French toast.

4 medium apples, cored, peeled, and chopped
25 dried apricots, cut in halves crosswise
1 cup dried fruit bits (diced dried fruit) any combination
1 bottle (750 ml) Cooper Vineyards Sweet Louisa (sweet red wine)
¾ cup water
1 cinnamon stick
Zest of half an orange
Juice of 1 orange
½ cup sugar
2 tablespoons honey

TO MAKE FRUIT COMPOTE:

- Mix apples, apricots, dried fruit bits, Cooper Vineyards Sweet Louisa wine, water, cinnamon, orange zest, orange juice, sugar, and honey in a Dutch oven or medium size pot.
- Bring to a boil; reduce heat to low and cook, uncovered for 45–60 minutes.
- The fruits will be tender and the liquid will be syrupy.
- Remove cinnamon stick.
- Serve warm or room temperature.
- Freeze or refrigerate to store.

Tortellini Chicken Salad with Sun-Dried Tomatoes

Advance preparation required

Serves 4
Preparation time: 30 minutes

Pair this recipe with Rockbridge Vineyard DeChiel Pinot Noir.

A hearty entrée salad.

SALAD

12 dehydrated sun-dried tomatoes
4 ounces cheese tortellini, cooked
4 ounces grilled chicken, diced
2 artichoke hearts, sliced
10 ounces fresh spinach, torn into pieces
2 ounces Feta cheese, crumbled
3 thin slices red onion, quartered

VINAIGRETTE DRESSING

2 cloves garlic
1 teaspoon dried oregano
1 tablespoon tomato paste
6 tablespoons balsamic vinegar
Salt and pepper to taste
½ cup olive oil

TO MAKE SALAD:

◆ Cover sun-dried tomatoes with boiling water and let sit for 30 minutes; cut into strips.

◆ Mix sun-dried tomato strips with tortellini, diced chicken, artichoke hearts, spinach, Feta cheese, and onion; toss together.

TO MAKE VINAIGRETTE DRESSING:

◆ Puree garlic, oregano, tomato paste, vinegar, salt, and pepper in a blender or food processor.

◆ Add oil with blender running; process until mixture is smooth.

◆ Mix enough dressing with the salad ingredients to moisten; toss to coat well.

SALAD DRESSING TIP:

◆ Try substituting beer for vinegar. The natural acidity of beer and the hop bitterness make it a great substitute for a new taste.

Margarita Melon Balls

Serves 6
Preparation time: 20 minutes

1 cup white tequila
1 cup fresh squeezed lime juice
¼ cup triple sec
2 tablespoons superfine sugar
8 cups melon balls (cantaloupe, honeydew, etc.)
Fresh mint to garnish

TO MAKE MELON BALLS:

◆ Whisk together white tequila, lime juice, triple sec, and superfine sugar.

◆ Arrange melon balls in a serving bowl.

◆ Pour liquid mixture over tops of melon balls.

◆ Garnish with mint.

Roast Chicken & Peach Salad

Serves 4

Preparation time: 30 minutes
Cooking time: 35 minutes

**Pair this recipe with
Tarara Vineyard & Winery Charvel.**

A completely different spinach salad.

BLACK OLIVE DRESSING

¼ cup pitted Calamata olives or other black brined olives

3 cloves garlic, peeled

1 tablespoon grainy mustard

1 tablespoon honey

¾ cup olive oil

¼ cup balsamic vinegar

Salt and freshly ground cracked black pepper to taste

SALAD

4 bone-in chicken breasts

Salt and pepper to taste

1 pound fresh spinach, stems removed, washed and dried

2 peaches, pitted and cut into 8 slices each

1 red bell pepper, seeded, cut into very thin strips

TO MAKE DRESSING:

◆ Mix olives, garlic, grainy mustard, and honey in a blender or food processor; puree.

◆ With motor running, pour olive oil into blender in a steady stream.

◆ Turn off motor; pour in balsamic vinegar, salt and pepper; pulse to blend.

TO MAKE SALAD:

◆ Preheat oven to 475 degrees.

◆ Rub chicken liberally with salt and pepper.

◆ Place chicken in roasting pan and cook for 35 minutes in a preheated 475 degree oven.

◆ Remove chicken from oven and cool.

◆ When chicken is cool enough to handle, use your hands to pull the meat off the bones.

◆ Cut meat into ½-inch-thick slices.

◆ Mix spinach, peaches, and red pepper in a large bowl.

◆ Stir the dressing.

◆ Pour just enough dressing over spinach to moisten the ingredients and toss to coat.

◆ Top with chicken and drizzle with dressing.

The Tidewater region is home to many colleges and universities. One of the oldest is Hampton University, located near Hampton's historic and picturesque waterfront. Established in 1868 during the days of Reconstruction, Hampton University is one of the nation's first black educational institutions. First named Hampton Normal and Agricultural Institute, its founding mission was to educate promising young African-American men and women to lead and teach the newly emancipated.

One of the most interesting historic features of the University is its Emancipation Oak. Standing proudly on the campus, this shady site was once a gathering spot where the formerly enslaved listened to the reading of the Emancipation Proclamation. Today, visitors may still find students congregating under the beautiful oak to discuss literature, politics, and the arts.

Another point of interest for the history hungry visitor is the Hampton University Museum. It houses collections of traditional African art, as well as Native American, Native Hawaiian, Pacific Island, and Asian art. The museum is the oldest African-American museum in the United States and one of the oldest museums in the Commonwealth of Virginia. The museum also features fine arts and objects relating to the history of the university.

Savory Spinach Salad

Serves **6**
Preparation time: 10 minutes

Pair this recipe with Horton Cellars Winery Cotes d'Orange.

The dressing for this salad also makes a good marinade.

10 ounces fresh baby spinach leaves
¼ pound bacon, cooked and crumbled
⅓ cup olive oil
¼ cup balsamic vinegar
¼ cup dry red wine
1 shallot, minced
1½ tablespoons brown sugar
½ cup pine nuts, toasted

TO MAKE SALAD:

◆ Place spinach leaves in serving bowl; sprinkle with bacon.
◆ Mix olive oil, balsamic vinegar, red wine, shallots, and brown sugar in a saucepan; bring to a boil.
◆ Remove from heat.
◆ Cover and let stand for five minutes.
◆ Pour dressing over spinach leaves and toss until spinach is wilted.
◆ Sprinkle with toasted pine nuts.

Tidewater Dressing

Serves **6**
Preparation time: 15 minutes

May be made in advance and stored in refrigerator.

¼ cup apple cider vinegar
4 teaspoons Dijon-style mustard or coarse grained mustard
2 tablespoons grated onion
¼ teaspoon thyme
2 cloves garlic, pressed
¼ teaspoon salt
¼ teaspoon ground pepper
½ cup extra virgin olive oil
¼ cup parsley

TO MAKE DRESSING:

◆ Mix apple cider vinegar, Dijon-style mustard, onion, thyme, garlic, salt, and pepper in bowl.
◆ Gradually add oil, beating constantly with wire whisk until thick.
◆ Stir in parsley.
◆ Toss with greens.

Smoked Turkey, Apple, & Walnut Salad

Advance preparation required

Serves 8
Preparation time: 25 minutes

**Pair this recipe with
Wintergreen Winery Chardonnay Monticello.**

A good entrée salad that is a great way
to use leftover turkey.

1 pound smoked turkey, cubed or shredded
1½ Granny Smith apples, diced
3 ribs celery, chopped
3 cups watercress, chopped
Salt and pepper to taste
4 tablespoons lemon juice
3 tablespoons Dijon-style mustard
1 egg yolk
1 teaspoon salt
1 teaspoon pepper
½ cup olive oil
½ head romaine lettuce
1 cup chopped walnuts, toasted
2 ounces crumbled goat cheese

TO MAKE SALAD:

◆ Mix smoked turkey, diced apples, chopped celery, and chopped watercress in a large bowl.
◆ Season with salt and pepper to taste.
◆ Mix lemon juice, Dijon-style mustard, egg yolk, salt, and pepper in a food processor until blended; gradually add oil to lemon juice mixture in a slow stream, processing until smooth and thick.
◆ Pour mixture over turkey mixture and toss gently.
◆ Cover and refrigerate for four hours.
◆ Mound salad on lettuce lined plate; sprinkle with walnuts and goat cheese.

Celebration Dressing

Advance preparation required

Yields 1½ cups
Preparation time: 15 minutes

Enjoy over one of many serving options: fresh
chopped vegetables, crisp green salad, baked
potatoes, or tortilla chips.

1 teaspoon lemon juice
1 tablespoon tarragon vinegar
½ cup sour cream
1 cup mayonnaise
¼ cup minced parsley
¼ teaspoon garlic salt
¼ teaspoon garlic powder
½ teaspoon minced chives
2 teaspoons anchovy paste
1 small onion, grated
Few sprinkles of chives

TO MAKE SALAD:

◆ Stir ingredients together; mix thoroughly.
◆ Chill for several hours.

Delightful Danish Coleslaw

Advance preparation required

Serves *8*

Preparation time: 20 minutes

Blue cheese is an amazing addition to the old standby. Blue cheese lovers take note.

2 tart apples, peeled, cored, and diced
1 tablespoon lemon juice
3 generous cups shredded cabbage
1 cup shredded purple cabbage
6 green onions, chopped
2 tablespoons fresh chives, chopped
¾ cup sour cream, lightly whipped
3 ounces blue cheese, crumbled
¼ cup mayonnaise
3 teaspoons white wine vinegar
1 teaspoon fresh dill, chopped
Salt to taste
2–3 grindings of pepper
Pinch of paprika

TO MAKE COLESLAW:

◆ Toss apples with lemon juice in a large bowl.
◆ Stir in cabbage, onions, chives, sour cream, blue cheese, mayonnaise, white vinegar, and dill; mix well and season with salt and pepper.
◆ Place salad in a serving bowl; sprinkle with paprika.
◆ Cover and refrigerate for several hours before serving.

Cucumber Slaw

Advance preparation required.

Serves *8*

Preparation time: 25 minutes

8 cups cucumbers, thinly sliced
1 medium onion, thinly sliced
1 tablespoon salt
1 cup white vinegar
2½ cups sugar
½ teaspoon crushed red pepper flakes

TO MAKE SLAW:

◆ Mix cucumbers, onion, and salt in a large glass bowl; toss to mix thoroughly.
◆ Cover and refrigerate for at least two hours and not longer than eight hours.
◆ Combine vinegar, sugar, and red pepper flakes; stir until sugar dissolves.
◆ Chill for several hours.
◆ Drain cucumbers in a colander, pressing lightly to remove excess water.
◆ Discard water.
◆ Place cucumber mixture in a new glass bowl, stir in dressing.
◆ Chill until ready to serve.

Red Potato Salad with Garlic Dressing

Advance preparation required.

Serves **6**

Preparation time: 20 minutes
Cooking time: 30 minutes

Flavor is best when left out
at room temperature.

6 cloves garlic, unpeeled
1 teaspoon vegetable oil
3 tablespoons red wine vinegar
1 teaspoon Dijon-style mustard
¾ teaspoon dried thyme
¼ teaspoon kosher salt
¼ teaspoon freshly ground black pepper
⅓ cup olive oil
2½ pounds small red potatoes
2 green onions, minced
1 medium red bell pepper, seeded and diced
¼ cup fresh minced parsley

TO MAKE SALAD:

◆ Preheat oven to 300 degrees.
◆ Toss garlic cloves with vegetable oil.
◆ Wrap the garlic tightly in a piece of aluminum foil; bake in preheated 300 degree oven for 30 minutes.
◆ Cool garlic.
◆ Cut tips of each garlic clove.
◆ Press garlic out of the skins into a food processor.
◆ Pour red wine vinegar, Dijon-style mustard, thyme, salt, and pepper into a food processor.
◆ Process to blend ingredients.
◆ Add olive oil to processor slowly until mixture is thickened and smooth.
◆ Transfer to another container, cover tightly, and refrigerate until ready to use.
◆ Place potatoes in a steamer basket and cook over boiling water, covered, for 25 minutes.
◆ Plunge potatoes into cold water and drain; set aside until cool enough to handle.
◆ Cut potatoes into quarters.
◆ Mix potatoes, green onion, red bell peppers, and parsley in a bowl.
◆ Stir in half of the dressing.
◆ Cover and refrigerate to marinate the potatoes.
◆ About two hours before serving, stir in remaining dressing.
◆ Do not return salad to refrigerator.
◆ Keep covered and leave at room temperature until ready to serve.

A trip to Portsmouth is an opportunity to discover just one of many unexpected surprises. Perhaps you will find a 64-seat planetarium, a restored lightship, or maybe even a building filled with ships, cannon balls, and uniforms. All of this and more can be found at Portsmouth's famous museums.

The Children's Museum of Virginia is Virginia's largest children's museum with more than 80 hands-on exhibits, including a chance to experience outer space. A restored lightship, commissioned in 1915 as a guide ship, is now known as the Lightship Museum. The lightship houses a wealth of maritime information near Portsmouth's waterfront. And our nation's oldest shipyard is home to the Portsmouth Naval Shipyard Museum. Here, you are able to investigate historic articles, model ships, cannon balls and weaponry, naval uniforms, and even a remnant of the Merrimac.

Seaside Scallop Salad

Serves **8**
Preparation time: 25 minutes
Cooking time: 3–4 minutes

Pair this recipe with First Colony Winery Blush.

1½ pounds scallops
3 cups shoe peg corn kernels
2 red bell peppers, seeded and diced
2 mangos, peeled, seeded and diced
1 avocado, diced
Juice of 2 lemons
Juice of 2 limes
8 cups mesclun greens
4 tablespoons chopped cilantro

TO MAKE SALAD:

◆ Spray a medium skillet with nonstick cooking spray; heat over medium heat.
◆ Cook the scallops until just opaque, approximately three to four minutes.
◆ Mix shoe peg corn, bell peppers, mangos, avocado, lemon, and lime juice in a medium bowl.
◆ Stir in the scallops; toss to combine.
◆ Divide the mesclun greens between eight plates and top with the scallop salad; garnish with cilantro.

North Mountain Winery's Raspberry Riesling Ranch Dressing

Yields **4** cups
Preparation time: 15 minutes

The tart/sweet flavors of this dressing are a real delight. North Mountain Vineyard & Winery Riesling is lightly sweet and very crisp, adding a lovely character. If a sweeter style Riesling is used, consider reducing the honey.

1 cup mayonnaise
1 cup sour cream
½ cup buttermilk
1 tablespoon fresh chopped garlic
1 teaspoon oregano
1 teaspoon onion powder
1 teaspoon celery seed
1 teaspoon dried basil leaves
½ teaspoon fresh dill weed
1 tablespoon fresh chives
1 tablespoon fresh chopped parsley
2 tablespoons grated Parmesan cheese
Dash hot pepper sauce
2 tablespoons raspberry vinegar
1 tablespoon Worcestershire sauce
1 teaspoon ground white pepper
2 tablespoons honey
¼ cup North Mountain Riesling
1 tablespoon Polaner™ All Fruit Seedless Raspberry

TO MAKE DRESSING:

◆ Mix ingredients in a bowl and whisk until smooth.
◆ Cover and chill in refrigerator for 30 minutes to allow the flavors to marry.
◆ Refrigerated and covered, this dressing will keep for one week.

Grilled Pear & Stilton

Serves 1
Preparation time: 10 minutes
Cooking time: 4 minutes

Pair this recipe with Jefferson Vineyards Chardonnay Reserve.

Multigrain bread can be substituted for the pecan raisin bread. This recipe is easily multiplied to feed more people.

2 tablespoons butter
2 slices raisin pecan bread
3–4 thin slices of pear
Stilton cheese, at room temperature

TO MAKE SANDWICH:

◆ Melt butter in a heavy skillet over medium-low heat.
◆ Place sliced pears on one slice of bread.
◆ Thinly spread Stilton cheese on second slice of bread.
◆ Press bread spread with Stilton cheese down on top of pears.
◆ Grill in melted butter over medium heat for two minutes per side or until cheese melts.

Virginia Tailgate Panini

Serves 4
Preparation time: 30 minutes
Cooking time: 10 minutes

Pair this recipe with Rockbridge Vineyard DeChiel Pinot Noir.

Make ahead, wrap in newspaper, and take to your tailgate party.

1 pound Virginia ham, thinly sliced
8 ounces provolone cheese, thinly sliced
2 medium tomatoes, sliced
8 ounces pepperoni, thinly sliced
¼ cup finely chopped red onion
¼ cup finely chopped black olives
¼ cup finely chopped green peppers
3 hard-cooked eggs, chopped
3 tablespoons olive oil
½ teaspoon balsamic vinegar
3 tablespoons tomato paste
1 tablespoon basil
2 tablespoons hot pepper sauce
Salt and pepper to taste
Panini or sourdough bread

TO MAKE SANDWICH:

◆ Preheat oven to 350 degrees.
◆ Set aside Virginia ham, provolone cheese, tomatoes, and pepperoni.
◆ Mix red onion, black olives, green peppers, hard-cooked eggs, olive oil, balsamic vinegar, tomato paste, basil, and hot pepper sauce in a large bowl.
◆ Stir in salt and pepper to taste.
◆ Layer Virginia ham, pepperoni, and three tablespoons of onion mixture on sliced panini bread.
◆ Top with provolone cheese, tomatoes, and bread.
◆ Wrap sandwich in foil; bake in preheated 350 degree oven for 10 minutes.

Gourmet Burgers

Serves 4
Preparation time: 45 minutes
Cooking time: 10–20 minutes for rolls,
8–10 minutes for hamburgers

**Pair this recipe with
Unicorn Winery Chambourcin.**

Also makes a wonderful meatloaf.

*Tip: For less grill mess,
finely chop or pulse cooled caramelized
onions in food processor before
incorporating into meat.*

1 onion, thinly sliced
1 teaspoon sugar
1 pound ground sirloin
1 teaspoon dried thyme
1 teaspoon dried rosemary
¼ to ½ teaspoon dried fennel
¼ teaspoon cayenne pepper
4 hamburger rolls
5.2 ounces Boursin™ cheese

TO MAKE BURGERS:

◆ Separate onions into rings.
◆ Place onions in a heavy skillet sprayed with nonstick butter-flavored cooking spray; cook covered over low heat for 20 minutes, stirring frequently.
◆ Remove cover and sprinkle sugar over onions; toss to coat.
◆ Return cover to skillet and cook an additional 20 minutes, stirring occasionally.
◆ Remove cover and cook an additional five minutes until the onions are caramelized and a golden brown color.
◆ Preheat oven to 150 degrees; heat hamburger rolls in preheated oven for 10–20 minutes.
◆ Mix caramelized onion, thyme, rosemary, fennel, cayenne pepper, and ground sirloin in a bowl.
◆ Shape meat mixture into four 5-ounce patties.
◆ Grill until internal temperature of meat reaches 160 degrees.
◆ Spread Boursin™ cheese over cooked hamburgers.

Tidewater Tortillas

Serves 4
Preparation time: 20 minutes

**Pair this recipe with
Chrysalis Vineyards Mariposa or
Hartwood Winery
Rappahannock Rose.**

This is a great brunch item
that you must make.

4 (8-inch) spinach tortillas
5.2 ounces Boursin™ cheese
4 ounces country cured Smithfield or Surry ham
4 eggs, scrambled and kept warm
4 ounces Brie cheese, rind removed, sliced
3–4 cups baby greens
3 tablespoons balsamic vinegar

TO MAKE TORTILLAS:

◆ Place tortillas on a flat surface.
◆ Spread Boursin™ cheese thinly over one side of tortilla.
◆ Divide ham evenly between tortillas to cover Boursin™ cheese.
◆ Sprinkle cooked eggs over ham.
◆ Place a layer of Brie cheese over eggs.
◆ Toss balsamic vinegar and greens in a small bowl.
◆ Place one cup of tossed greens with dressing on each tortilla.
◆ Roll up tortilla and enjoy.

Decadent Brie & Bacon Croissant

Serves 1
Preparation time: 15 minutes
Cooking time: 10 minutes

Pair this recipe with Kluge Estate Winery & Vineyard Sparkling Brut Wine.

Treat yourself and guests
to this great weekend lunch.

Croissant (1 per person)
Slices of Brie cheese (to cover croissant), rind removed
2 slices of cooked bacon per person

TO MAKE SANDWICH:

◆ Preheat oven to 300 degrees.

◆ Slice croissant horizontally in half.

◆ Place bacon on one side of croissant.

◆ Place sliced Brie cheese on top of bacon.

◆ Bake in preheated 300 degree oven, open faced for 10 minutes or until Brie cheese melts; watch closely.

◆ Place top and bottom of croissant together; serve hot.

Greek Burgers

Serves 4
Preparation time: 15 minutes
Cooking time: For beef, the internal temperature should be 145 degrees for rare, 160 degrees for medium, and 170 degrees for well-done; for lamb, the internal temperature should be 175 degrees; and for turkey, the internal temperature should be 165 degrees.

Pair this recipe with Horton Cellars Winery Norton.

A little Mediterranean flavor
brought to Virginia.

1 pound lean ground beef, turkey or lamb
1 onion, chopped
1 teaspoon oregano
½ teaspoon black pepper
2 ounces Feta cheese, crumbled
1 tablespoon lemon juice
Olive oil
Rolls
Roasted red peppers

TO MAKE BURGERS:

◆ Mix ground meat, onion, oregano, black pepper, Feta cheese, and lemon juice.

◆ Divide meat mixture; form into four hamburger patties.

◆ Brush hamburgers with olive oil and grill until desired doneness.

◆ Serve on rolls with roasted red peppers.

Epicurean White Pizza

Advance preparation required.

Serves 4
Preparation time: 40 minutes
Cooking time: 13 minutes

Pair this recipe with Oasis Winery Reserve Cabernet Sauvignon.

The combination of cheeses is spectacular.

Pizza stone
½ pound yellow onion, thinly sliced
1 tablespoon sugar
1 sheet puff pastry, thawed
4 ounces Virginia Gouda cheese, shredded
4 ounces Fontina cheese, shredded
4 ounces mozzarella cheese, shredded
2 tablespoons butter
⅓ cup slivered almonds
2 tablespoons minced garlic
10 ounces fresh spinach

TO MAKE PIZZA:

- Place pizza stone in oven and heat oven to 400 degrees.
- Spray a heavy skillet with nonstick butter-flavored cooking spray; heat over low heat.
- Separate onions into rings and place in heated skillet.
- Cover and cook for 20 minutes, stirring occasionally.
- Remove cover and sprinkle onions with sugar; stir to coat.
- Return cover to skillet and cook onions for an additional 20 minutes, stirring occasionally.
- Remove cover and cook for an additional five minutes until onions are golden brown and caramelized.
- Roll out puff pastry on lightly floured surface to 12 by 15 inches.
- Transfer pastry to a cookie sheet.
- Slightly turn edges over.
- Prick bottom, but not the edges, of the pastry with a fork.
- Mix Gouda, Fontina, and mozzarella cheeses; sprinkle evenly over the pastry.
- Melt butter; add almonds and cook until lightly brown.
- Stir in garlic and continue cooking over low heat; watch carefully so that it does not burn.
- Remove spinach stems and tear into small pieces; place in a large pot.
- Add ¼ cup water to pot over low heat; let spinach wilt, stirring occasionally.
- Remove spinach from the heat; squeeze out excess water with a potato ricer or in a towel.
- Add spinach to almond garlic mixture; mix well.
- Place spinach mixture on top of cheese.
- Sprinkle with caramelized onions.
- Spray edges of pastry with olive oil cooking spray.
- Place baking sheet with pizza on top of pizza stone in preheated 400 degree oven.
- Cook 13–14 minutes or until cheese melts and pastry is golden brown.

Chesapeake Bay Ham & Cheese Pizza

Advance preparation required.

Serves 4
Preparation time: 35 minutes
Cooking time: 13 minutes

Pair this recipe with Breaux Vineyards Cabernet Sauvignon.

Gourmet pizza made at home.

1 pound onions, thinly sliced
1 tablespoon sugar
1 sheet puff pastry, thawed
6 ounces Fontina cheese, shredded
5 ounces Virginia Gouda cheese, shredded
1 teaspoon garlic powder
1 tablespoon fresh rosemary, crushed, or 1 teaspoon dried rosemary, crushed
1 tablespoon fresh thyme leaves, or 1 teaspoon dried thyme
¼ teaspoon ground sage
4 ounces country cured Smithfield ham, cut into bite-size pieces

TO MAKE PIZZA:

- Spray a heavy skillet with nonstick butter flavored cooking spray; heat over low heat.
- Separate onions into rings and place in heated skillet.
- Cover and cook for 20 minutes, stirring occasionally.
- Remove cover and sprinkle onions with sugar; stir to coat.
- Return cover to skillet and cook onions for an additional 20 minutes, stirring occasionally.
- Remove cover and cook for an additional five minutes until onions are golden brown and caramelized.
- Preheat oven to 400 degrees.
- Roll out puff pastry, on a lightly floured surface, to 15 by 12 inches; transfer to a baking sheet.
- Roll edges slightly to form an edge or crimp like a pie dough.
- Prick the entire surface of the puff pastry using a fork.
- Spray puff pastry with olive oil cooking spray.
- Distribute caramelized onions evenly on top of puff pastry.
- Mix Fontina and Gouda cheeses with garlic powder, rosemary, thyme, and sage in a bowl.
- Place cheese mixture on top of onions.
- Scatter ham on top of cheese.
- Bake in preheated 400 degree oven for 13 minutes or until cheese is melted and the crust is golden brown.

NOTE: Can be made ahead. Cover with foil and refrigerate up to four hours. Bring back to room temperature before baking.

Pasta

Gatherings Menu

(Family gatherings, reunions, graduations)

◆

Southern Shrimp Cakes or

St. George Brewery's Drunken Shrimp Overboard

Pair with Horton Cellars Winery Manseng or

St. George Porter or

Alpenglow Classic Blush Sparkling Cider

◆

Savory Spinach Salad

Valhalla's Summer Linguini

Pair with Horton Cellars Winery Cotes d'Orange

◆

Balsamic Chicken and Mushrooms or

Bayside Balsamic-Glazed Salmon

Pair with First Colony Winery Cabernet Franc or

Barboursville Vineyards Brut

◆

Mermaid's Margarita Pie

Enjoy with coffee!

May we remain an unbroken circle,
continually strengthened by the bond of love we share.
One generation entwined with another—
always teaching, learning, and growing into our shared future.

—*Toast written by Vickie Madison, JLNVB member*

Section photograph underwritten by:
Hampton Roads Magazine

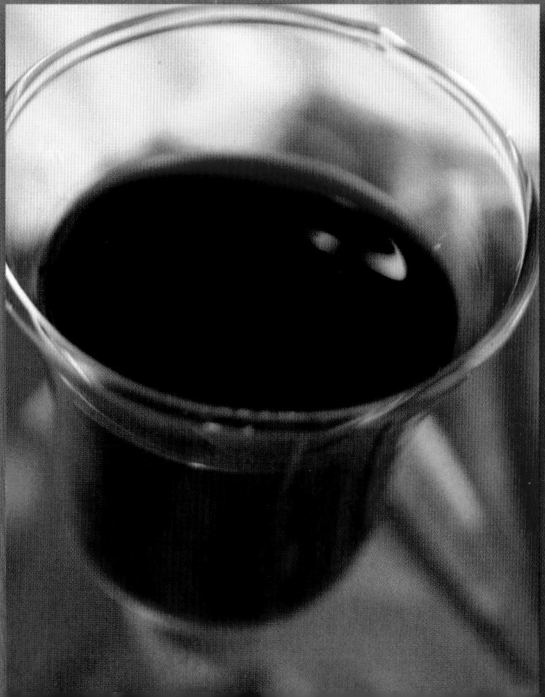

Residents of Franklin and Southampton County enjoy small town life in an area rich in history and tradition. There are many sights and smells in this neck of the woods, just 60 miles west of Virginia Beach.

There's the smell of International Paper, the paper mill that locals jokingly say, "smells like money." Originally Camp Manufacturing Company and then Union Camp Corporation, the paper mill has been the leading industry in the area since its founding in the late 1800s. With acres and acres of woodlands and two flowing rivers, the area was an ideal location for the mill.

There's also the smell of freshly dug Virginia jumbo peanuts. As you drive down the back roads in the county, there's no mistaking the "earthy" smell in the crisp autumn air at harvest time. Southampton County leads the state in peanut production and is one of the state's biggest agricultural counties.

And then there's the smell of food wafting from Fred's Restaurant on Main Street, a longstanding Franklin landmark. Locals gather here to discuss many things, including the big football game between continuing rivals Franklin High and Southampton High, local politics, or happenings "over at the mill."

Valhalla's Summer Linguini

Advance preparation required.

Serves **8**
Preparation time: 15 minutes

**Pair this recipe with
Valhalla Vineyards Dry Rose.**

For a change of pace, add fresh shrimp (when in season) or artichoke hearts.

4 large tomatoes, chopped
8 ounces Brie, Feta, or goat cheese, chopped
1 cup chopped fresh basil
5 cloves garlic, pressed
½ cup olive oil
½ teaspoon salt
½ teaspoon pepper
16 ounces linguine, cooked, drained, and kept hot
Parmesan cheese

TO MAKE PASTA:

◆ Mix tomatoes, cheese, basil, and garlic in a large bowl.
◆ Whisk together olive oil, salt, and pepper.
◆ Pour dressing over tomato mixture; toss gently to coat.
◆ Let stand, covered, at room temperature for one hour or longer.
◆ Cook linguine and drain. Keep hot.
◆ Toss hot pasta with tomato mixture.
◆ Sprinkle with Parmesan cheese and pepper to taste.

Rustic Red Sauce

Yields **5** cups
Preparation time: 20 minutes
Cooking time: 30 minutes

This sauce is thick and flavorful to taste.

2 tablespoons olive oil
1½ cups finely chopped onions
½ cup finely chopped carrots
3 cloves garlic, minced
½ cup dehydrated sun-dried tomatoes, softened with boiling water
½ cup red wine
1 teaspoon dried basil
1 teaspoon dried oregano
1 teaspoon dried marjoram
2 pounds roma tomatoes, seeded, pulped, and chopped
1 can (16 ounces) tomato sauce
1 tablespoon sugar, optional if using a sweet red wine

TO MAKE SAUCE:

◆ Heat olive oil in a large skillet over medium-low heat; stir in onions and carrots.
◆ Cook for five minutes, or until onions are soft.
◆ Stir in garlic and re-hydrated sun-dried tomatoes; cook for four minutes.
◆ Stir in red wine, basil, oregano, marjoram, chopped tomatoes, tomato sauce, and sugar.
◆ Cover and cook over low heat for 30 minutes.
◆ Let cool.
◆ Purée cooled mixture in blender.

Pasta with Savory Sausage & Cream

Serves 4
Preparation time: 30 minutes
Cooking time: 20 minutes

**Pair this recipe with
Ingleside Plantation Vineyards or
Barboursville Vineyards Chardonnay.**

You can substitute lower-fat ingredients or vegetarian sausage for a healthier alternative.

1 tablespoon olive oil
¼ cup sun-dried tomatoes in oil, drained and oil reserved
1 tablespoon oil from sun-dried tomatoes
½ cup diced yellow onions
3 medium cloves garlic, peeled and diced
1 pound sweet Italian sausage
½ teaspoon crushed red pepper
28 ounces Italian-style plum tomatoes, drained and chopped
1½ cups whipping cream
½ teaspoon salt
8 ounces bowtie pasta
¼ cup minced fresh wide-leaf parsley or basil
½ cup pine nuts, toasted
Feta or Gorgonzola cheese

TO MAKE PASTA:

◆ Heat olive oil and reserved sun-dried tomato oil in a large skillet; mix in onions and garlic and cook until tender.
◆ Stir sausage, sun-dried tomatoes, and red pepper into olive and onion mixture.
◆ Cook for seven minutes, breaking up sausage until no longer pink.
◆ Stir in tomatoes, whipping cream, and salt.
◆ Lower heat and simmer until mixture thickens, approximately four minutes.
◆ Cook bowtie pasta in boiling water with salt, approximately 10 minutes or until al dente.
◆ Drain water; stir bowtie pasta into sauce.
◆ Simmer for an additional two minutes.
◆ Stir in parsley or basil.
◆ Serve with toasted pine nuts and the cheese of your choice.

from Rebec Vineyards:

Good for What Aioli's You

Advance preparation required.

Serves **8**
Preparation time: 30 minutes
Cooking time: 55 minutes

**Pair this recipe with
Rebec Vineyards Viognier.**

This pasta has been a winner at the
Virginia Garlic Festival
held every year in October
at Rebec Vineyards.

2 heads garlic
4 tablespoons olive oil, divided
¼ teaspoon salt
¼ teaspoon pepper
1 large Vidalia onion, thinly sliced
½ ounce dried porcini mushrooms, soaked in water for 30 minutes, or 3 ounces fresh porcini mushrooms
16 ounces bowtie pasta, cooked and drained
½ cup white wine
1 tablespoon butter, ice cold, cut into pieces
5 basil leaves, thinly sliced

TO MAKE PASTA:

◆ Preheat oven to 350 degrees.
◆ Slice off top half of garlic heads.
◆ Place garlic heads in a small ovenproof dish and pour 2 tablespoons olive oil over tops; sprinkle garlic heads with salt and pepper.
◆ Cover and roast garlic heads in 350 degree oven until golden, approximately 45 minutes.
◆ Cool roasted garlic and remove peel.
◆ Heat remaining 2 tablespoons olive oil in a large skillet.
◆ Mix in onion and cover skillet; cook slowly over low heat to caramelize, stirring occasionally for approximately 30–45 minutes.
◆ Uncover skillet and finish onions to a deep caramel color over medium heat.
◆ While onions are cooking, prepare bowtie pasta.
◆ Stir drained mushrooms into caramelized onions and cook for five minutes.
◆ Add roasted garlic cloves; cook for five minutes.
◆ Pour white wine into pan and cook, scraping bottom of pan to loosen any food particles.
◆ Stir and boil for one minute; remove from heat.
◆ Stir in butter.
◆ Stir cooked bowtie into hot garlic and mushroom sauce; toss to combine.
◆ Serve garnished with slices of basil.

Breaux Vineyards' All-Time-Favorite Puttanesca Sauce

Serves 4
Preparation time: 15 minutes
Cooking time: 20 minutes

Pair this recipe with Breaux Vineyards Lafayette Cabernet Franc.

The origination of Puttanesca is quite colorful, like the sauce.

8 cloves garlic, peeled and finely chopped
2 tablespoons anchovy paste
1/4 cup extra virgin olive oil
35 ounces peeled plum tomatoes, drained and cut in quarters
1 jar (2.5 ounces) capers, drained and rinsed
1 1/2 cups of pitted Calamata olives, coarsely chopped
1/8 teaspoon dried red pepper flakes
Coarsely ground black pepper to taste

TO MAKE SAUCE:

◆ Place garlic, anchovy paste, and olive oil in heavy cast iron skillet.
◆ Mash everything together over medium heat.
◆ Add plum tomatoes, capers, Calamata olives, red pepper flakes, and black pepper to skillet and heat to simmering, stirring frequently.
◆ Reduce heat and continue to simmer uncovered until sauce has thickened to your liking, stirring occasionally.
◆ Serve over cooked spaghetti.

Sun-Dried Tomatoes & Walnuts with Penne Pasta

Serves 4
Preparation time: 30 minutes
Cooking time: 10–15 minutes

Pair this recipe with Tarara Vineyard & Winery Meritage.

Cooking the walnuts gives this dish a nice crunch.

4 tablespoons olive oil
2/3 cup green onions, chopped
1/4 cup walnuts, chopped
1/4 cup sun-dried tomatoes packed in oil, drained and sliced
12 ounces penne pasta, cooked and drained
2 ounces Feta cheese, crumbled
1/2 cup whipping cream
4 tablespoons Romano cheese
Freshly ground white pepper

TO MAKE PASTA:

◆ Heat olive oil in large skillet, add green onions and walnuts, and cook over medium heat for five minutes.
◆ Stir sun-dried tomatoes into skillet and cook an additional two minutes.
◆ Add cooked penne pasta and Feta cheese to sun-dried tomato mixture.
◆ Reduce heat to low; stir gently until cheese melts.
◆ Stir whipping cream and Romano cheese into pasta.
◆ Season with white pepper.
◆ Stir well and serve.

Artichoke Onion Pasta

Serves **6**

Preparation time: 20 minutes
Cooking time: 15 minutes

Pair this recipe with Barboursville Vineyards Sangiovese Reserve.

Serve this pasta with grilled or baked chicken, or dice chicken breast and toss with pasta.

1 large onion, chopped fine
4 large cloves garlic, chopped
1 (7 ounce) jar marinated artichoke hearts, chopped, reserve 3 tablespoons of liquid
28 ounces diced tomatoes
1 teaspoon oregano
½ cup prepared pesto
¼ teaspoon salt
12 ounces penne pasta, cooked and drained
2 ounces freshly grated Parmesan cheese

TO MAKE PASTA:

◆ Cook onion and garlic in reserved artichoke liquid for six to seven minutes until tender.

◆ Mix tomato, artichoke, and oregano into onion mixture.

◆ Simmer for eight minutes; add prepared pesto and salt and heat for one additional minute.

◆ Serve over hot penne pasta with Parmesan cheese.

Greek Shrimp & Pasta

Serves **8**

Preparation time: 25 minutes
Cooking time: 5 minutes

Pair this recipe with North Mountain Vineyard & Winery Chardonnay.

May easily substitute chicken for shrimp.

½ cup olive oil
8 teaspoons minced garlic
2 pounds medium shrimp, peeled and deveined
4 cups canned artichoke hearts, drained and chopped
16 ounces crumbled Feta cheese
1 cup chopped fresh tomato
6 tablespoons fresh lemon juice
6 tablespoons fresh parsley
4 tablespoons fresh oregano
1 teaspoon pepper
½ teaspoon salt
16 ounces angel hair pasta, cooked, drained, and kept warm

TO MAKE PASTA:

◆ Heat olive oil over medium heat in a skillet; add garlic and shrimp.

◆ Cook for at least two minutes.

◆ Mix in artichoke hearts, Feta cheese, tomatoes, lemon juice, parsley, oregano, pepper, and salt.

◆ Cook an additional two minutes or until shrimp are cooked.

◆ Serve over cooked angel hair pasta.

Cooper Vineyards' Wild Mushroom Ragout

Serves 6
Preparation time: 15 minutes
Cooking time: 30 minutes

Pair this recipe with Cooper Vineyards Coopertage Blanc.

Serve this over pasta.

1 tablespoon olive oil
⅓ cup finely diced onion
1 clove garlic, minced
½ teaspoon grated lemon rind
1 cup Cooper Vineyards Chardonnay
½ cup chicken broth
3 tablespoons sour cream
2 teaspoons flour
½ cup olive oil
5 cups fresh mushrooms (white button, cremini, portobello, or shiitake), stems removed
3 tablespoons minced fresh herbs (chives, parsley), divided
2 tablespoons Cooper Vineyards Chardonnay
3 tablespoons grated Parmesan cheese

TO MAKE RAGOUT:

◆ Heat olive oil in a skillet.
◆ Stir in onions and garlic and cook until translucent.
◆ Stir in lemon peel, Cooper Vineyards Chardonnay, and chicken broth.
◆ Boil until liquid is reduced in volume by half, approximately ¾ cup.
◆ Lower heat.
◆ Mix sour cream and flour; stir into reduced wine liquid; simmer until mixture starts to thicken.
◆ Remove from heat and set aside.
◆ Heat olive oil in a large skillet; stir in mushrooms, cook until tender.
◆ Grill and dice if using portobello mushrooms.
◆ Mix cooked mushrooms and reduced wine; season to taste with salt and pepper.
◆ Stir in 1 tablespoon of fresh herbs and 2 tablespoons of Cooper Vineyards Chardonnay.
◆ The dish can be refrigerated at this point.
◆ Reheat before serving and garnish with remaining herbs and Parmesan cheese.

Evenings in Portsmouth provide many opportunities for entertainment, as the city is home to several theaters and facilities. The Commodore Theatre, a restored 1945 movie theater, features a 42-foot screen, an updated sound system, and crystal chandeliers. Guests can enjoy dinner in this charming atmosphere while viewing current films.

Another option for nightlife in Portsmouth is the NTELOS Pavilion at Harbor Center, a large outdoor concert venue with space for 6,500 guests. This waterfront pavilion boasts a wide variety of performances each concert season. Willett Hall, a 2,000-seat entertainment hall, offers dance performances, concerts, speakers, and plays. Portsmouth Community Concerts organizes many events at Willett Hall, inviting participation from the entire community. Many local eateries even provide "concert cuisine" discounts to theater patrons in support of the performing arts.

Whether you want to take in a show, listen to a classical concerto, or watch the stars come alive while your favorite band hits the stage, Portsmouth has just the ticket to your entertainment of choice.

Worth It Spinach Lasagna

Serves 12
Preparation time: 60 minutes
Cooking time: 1 hour, 20 minutes

**Pair this recipe with
The Williamsburg Winery
Two Shilling Red.**

You can substitute prepared sauce, but the extra effort it takes to make fresh sauce is worth the time.

1 can (28 ounces) whole tomatoes, drained and juice saved
¼ cup balsamic vinegar
¼ cup water
¼ cup sugar
1 tablespoon olive oil
1 cup chopped carrots
1 cup chopped onion
1 cup chopped celery
1 can (14.5 ounces) diced tomatoes, drained
1 tablespoon minced garlic
½ cup white wine
1 tablespoon tomato paste
8 ounces sliced mushrooms
20 ounces baby spinach, cleaned and stems removed
Dash of nutmeg
32 ounces ricotta cheese
2 eggs, lightly beat
1 ounce Parmesan cheese
1 tablespoon garlic powder
16 ounces Muenster cheese, shredded
9 oven-ready, no-boil lasagna noodles

TO MAKE LASAGNA:

◆ Mix juice from whole tomatoes, balsamic vinegar, water, and sugar in a small saucepan; bring to a boil.

◆ Reduce heat and simmer until thick and syrupy, approximately 20–30 minutes.

◆ Heat olive oil in a large skillet over medium-low heat; add carrots, onions, and celery; cook until soft.

◆ Break whole tomatoes in a bowl and remove seeds (seeds will make the sauce bitter).

◆ Mix whole tomatoes and diced tomatoes; add to onion mixture.

◆ Mix minced garlic, white wine, and tomato paste; add to tomato mixture and bring liquid to a boil.

◆ Reduce heat to medium low; cook until thickened, approximately 10–15 minutes.

◆ Add balsamic vinegar mixture when sauce is thick; stir thoroughly.

◆ Meanwhile, place mushrooms in a nonstick skillet.

◆ Cover skillet; cook mushrooms over low heat until soft.

◆ Remove cover and let any liquid from the mushrooms evaporate.

◆ Remove mushrooms from heat; stir mushrooms into tomato mixture.

◆ Place spinach in a large pot; sprinkle with nutmeg.

◆ Pour ⅓ cup water over spinach; cover and cook over low heat until soft and wilted.

◆ Drain spinach completely—use a potato ricer if you have one. You want all the liquid in the spinach removed.

Continued on next page...

continued from page 70, TO MAKE LASAGNA:

- Chop spinach slightly.
- Preheat oven to 375 degrees.
- Mix ricotta cheese, eggs, Parmesan cheese, and garlic powder.
- Stir drained spinach into ricotta mixture; stir until blended.
- Lightly grease 13 X 9 X 2 baking dish.
- Cover bottom of dish with one-half of tomato sauce mixture.
- Place a layer of oven-ready, no-boil lasagna noodles on top of sauce.
- Top with ricotta and spinach mixture.
- Top with a layer of Muenster cheese.
- Repeat, starting again with the tomato sauce and ending with Muenster cheese.
- Cover with aluminum foil.
- The lasagna can be refrigerated at this point; if so, bring back to room temperature before baking.
- Bake in preheated 375 degree oven for 80 minutes.
- Remove from oven and let stand for 10 minutes before serving.

Black Bean Lasagna

Serves 10
Preparation time: 30 minutes
Cooking time: 1 hour 15 minutes

Pair this recipe with Chateau Morrisette Cabernet Franc.

Suitable for entertaining guests or family dinners.

8 ounces tomato sauce
15 ounces black beans, drained
14 ounces stewed tomatoes with juice, coarsely chopped
8 ounces mushrooms, sliced
1 large onion, chopped
9 oven-ready, no-boil lasagna noodles
6 cups fresh spinach, chopped
24 ounces cottage cheese
4 ounces Parmesan cheese, shredded
8 ounces shredded mozzarella cheese

TO MAKE LASAGNA:

- Preheat oven to 350 degrees.
- Mix tomato sauce, black beans, and stewed tomatoes in a bowl.
- Spray skillet with nonstick cooking spray and cook mushrooms and onions until translucent.
- Spray 13 X 9 X 2 baking dish with nonstick cooking spray.
- Layer three to four oven-ready, no-boil lasagna noodles in bottom of baking dish.
- Cover noodles with half of tomato and bean mixture; then layer, in this order, half of spinach, half of mushroom mixture, and half of cottage cheese.
- Sprinkle with half of Parmesan cheese.
- Repeat layers.
- Cover tightly with foil and bake in preheated 350 degree oven for 60 minutes.
- Uncover and bake an additional 15 minutes, top with mozzarella cheese and return to oven for five minutes.
- Let stand five minutes before serving.

Welcome Home Menu

(Hails and Farewells)

◆

Coastal Crab and Brie Bites
Pair with Williamsburg Pale Ale™

◆

Mixed Greens with
North Mountain Vineyards' Raspberry Riesling Ranch Dressing

◆

Grilled Veal Chops with Grape Chutney from Barboursville Vineyards
Asiago Chive Mashed Potatoes
Baked Wild Mushrooms with Basil and Garlic
Pair with Barboursville Vineyards Sangiovese Reserve

◆

No Bake Chocolate Delicacy
Enjoy with coffee!

*Here's to the pain of goodbye,
If only because it is matched by the gaiety of hello.
Here's to love,
An emotion that knows no distance.
Here's to friendship,
The value of which cannot be weighed or surpassed.
May your farewells be short and few,
And your greetings heartfelt and joyous.*

—Toast written by Anne McPhee, JLNVB member

Section photograph dedicated to:
Tidewater/Hampton Roads Area

from Barboursville Vineyards:

Grilled Veal Chops with Grape Chutney

Serves **8**
Preparation time: 20 minutes
Cooking time: 16 minutes

Pair this recipe with Barboursville Vineyards Sangiovese Reserve.

If you can find other rich red grapes, such as a merlot or cabernet grape, use them. Some specialty grocery stores carry other grape varieties besides table grapes. If you do use the other varieties, make sure you slice them in half and remove the seeds.

This goes well with soft polenta and wilted spinach. Pork chops are a good substitute.

1 bunch seedless red grapes, sliced in half, weighing approximately 1½ pounds
¼ cup Barboursville Vineyards red wine
2 tablespoons balsamic vinegar
2 tablespoons sugar
½ cup chopped walnuts, toasted
Salt and pepper to taste
8 veal chops, bone-in, weighing approximately 10 ounces each
Olive oil to taste
Salt and pepper to taste

TO MAKE VEAL:

◆ Heat heavy bottom saucepan over medium heat.

◆ Toss grapes into saucepan; cook for one to two minutes.

◆ Stir in red wine, balsamic vinegar, and sugar; cook for seven minutes.

◆ Stir in walnuts and season with salt and pepper; keep warm.

◆ Heat grill to medium-high heat (for gas grills) or glowing coals (for charcoal grills).

◆ Coat each veal chop with olive oil; season with salt and pepper.

◆ Place veal chops on grill; cook on each side for five to seven minutes for medium doneness.

◆ The veal chops can be cooked less or more depending on your desired doneness.

◆ Spoon grape chutney over veal chops; serve immediately.

Virginia Veal

Serves 2
Preparation time: 15 minutes
Cooking time: 10 minutes

Pair this recipe with Stonewall Vineyards & Winery Chambourcin or Oasis Winery Sparkling Brut Wine.

Lovely for a romantic dinner.

10 ounces fresh spinach
⅓ cup water
2 veal cutlets or scaloppini, approximately 2 ounces each
Flour for dredging
1 tablespoon butter
2 tablespoons olive oil
½ cup dry sherry
1 small shallot, diced
4 slices Brie (rind removed) or Gouda cheese, thinly sliced
　to cover meat

TO MAKE VEAL:

◆ Heat a large pot over medium heat; place spinach in pot with water; cover and cook for two minutes. Do not let water boil away; add more water if necessary.
◆ Squeeze spinach dry.
◆ Pound veal cutlets lightly to uniform thickness.
◆ Dredge veal cutlets in flour to coat veal lightly.
◆ Melt butter in cast iron skillet over medium-high heat.
◆ Stir in olive oil; heat until bubbly and butter begins to brown.
◆ Place veal cutlets in skillet and cook one minute per side.
◆ Remove veal cutlets to warm plate; cover to keep warm.
◆ Remove skillet from stove and pour in sherry; return skillet to stove.
◆ Bring sherry to a boil while scraping bottom of skillet to incorporate the fond; stir in shallots.
◆ Break up spinach; stir into skillet.
◆ Stir spinach and sherry to combine.
◆ When the sherry is absorbed into the spinach, flatten it out.
◆ Return veal cutlets to the pan; place on spinach and cover with Brie or Gouda cheese.
◆ Cover skillet; take off the heat.
◆ Allow cheese to melt, approximately two minutes.

Lamb in Puff Pastry

Advance preparation required.

Serves *8*
Preparation time: 50 minutes
Cooking time: 17 minutes

Pair this recipe with Tarara Vineyard & Winery Meritage or North Mountain Vineyard & Winery Chambourcin.

This recipe can also be made using filet mignon.

LAMB
3–4 pounds boneless leg of lamb
4 cloves garlic, chopped
6 tablespoons bourbon
4 tablespoons vegetable oil
4 tablespoons soy sauce
4 small slivers fresh gingerroot
2 tablespoons oil
Salt and pepper to taste

DUXELLES
½ medium onion, finely chopped
2 tablespoons butter
½ pound mushrooms, finely chopped
1 clove garlic, crushed
Salt and pepper to taste
Tarragon to taste
2 puff pastry sheets, thawed
1 egg, beaten
½ teaspoon salt
8 slices prosciutto, cut into 16 pieces 2 inches round

TO MAKE LAMB:
◆ Roll lamb out into a nonreactive pan.
◆ Combine garlic, bourbon, vegetable oil, soy sauce, and fresh ginger to make marinade.
◆ Pour marinade over lamb; refrigerate covered for 8–12 hours.
◆ Remove lamb from marinade.
◆ Cut lamb into eight ¾-inch thick steaks.
◆ Heat oil in skillet over high heat; sear lamb steaks for 30 seconds per side.
◆ Season with salt and pepper.
◆ Set lamb aside to cool.

TO MAKE DUXELLES:
◆ Cook onions slowly in butter in a large skillet until soft but not browned.
◆ Stir in mushrooms; cook over medium heat, stirring until all moisture is evaporated.
◆ Stir in garlic and cook an additional 30 seconds.
◆ Stir in salt, pepper, and tarragon to taste; set aside to cool.

TO ASSEMBLE:
◆ Roll out thawed puff pastry sheets on a lightly floured surface to two sheets each measuring 16 by 18 inches.
◆ Cut each puff pastry sheet in half, crosswise.
◆ Mix egg and salt; brush half of puff pastry with egg mixture.

Continued on next page...

continued from page 76:

TO ASSEMBLE:

◆ Set four pieces of prosciutto on puff pastry in two parallel lines, about 1 inch from the edge.

◆ Spread Duxelles over each piece of prosciutto.

◆ Top Duxelles with lamb steak.

◆ Spread remaining Duxelles over lamb steaks; top with remaining prosciutto.

◆ Cover lamb steaks with second sheet of puff pastry, allowing it to fall loosely down between the steaks.

◆ Using a ball of pastry dipped in flour, press down firmly to seal the dough around the steaks.

◆ Cut around each lamb steak with a pastry wheel, leaving a ½-inch border.

◆ Press the edges of puff pastry to seal.

◆ Brush with egg-salt mixture.

◆ Place puff pastry filled with lamb on greased baking sheet.

◆ Pile the dough trimmings one on top of the other and roll out to a thin sheet.

◆ Cut decorations out with a cookie cutter or with a paring knife and decorate each of the steaks.

◆ Brush puff pastry surface with egg mixture.

◆ Make a hole in the center of puff pastry with the point of a knife to allow the steam to escape.

◆ Chill the steaks at least 15 minutes.

◆ The chops can be prepared up to this point and stored in the refrigerator for up to eight hours.

◆ Preheat oven to 450 degrees.

◆ Bake in preheated oven on a heavy baking sheet until pastry is well browned, approximately 12–15 minutes for rare and 15–17 minutes for medium to well-done.

◆ Serve at once.

from Chateau Morrisette:
Sesame Grilled Beef with Pear Dipping Sauce

Advance preparation required.

Serves 4–6
Preparation time: 30 minutes
Cooking time: 5 minutes

Pair this recipe with Chateau Morrisette Our Dog Blue.

Serve the meat wrapped in lettuce as a heavy hors d'oeuvres.

BEEF
2 pounds sirloin steak, sliced across the grain 1/4 inch thick
½ cup soy sauce
⅓ cup sugar
4 tablespoons dry sherry
3 green onions, minced
5 cloves garlic, mashed
2 tablespoons sesame oil
Juice of half an orange
2 tablespoons toasted sesame seeds
½ teaspoon fresh ground black pepper

PEAR DIPPING SAUCE
1 cup soy sauce
½ cup sake
½ cup mirin
2 Asian pears, peeled, cored and finely chopped
4 green onions, finely chopped
½ cup yellow onions, finely minced or grated
4 tablespoons toasted sesame seeds

TO MAKE BEEF:
- Pound sliced meat between sheets of plastic wrap to make thin strips.
- Mix soy sauce, sugar, dry sherry, green onions, garlic, sesame oil, orange juice, sesame seeds, and black pepper; stir to dissolve the sugar.
- Place meat in the marinade, turning the meat once or twice, and marinate up to two hours.
- Grill over hot coals for one to two minutes per side or cook under a broiler if no grill is available, making sure the meat is turned midway.
- Serve warm with green leaf lettuce leaves and Pear Dipping Sauce.
- To eat, wrap meat in lettuce leaf like a small package; dip into sauce.

TO MAKE SAUCE:
- Mix soy sauce, sake, mirin, Asian pears, green onions, yellow onions, and sesame seeds and let flavors meld at room temperature for 30 minutes before serving.

Snappy Roast

Advance preparation required.

Serves 8
Preparation time: 45 minutes
Cooking time: 2 hours

**Pair this recipe with
Barboursville Vineyards Pinot Noir.**

3½ pounds rump roast, trimmed
2 cups water
1 cup red wine vinegar
1 medium onion, sliced
6 whole cloves
4 peppercorns, crushed
1½ teaspoons salt
1 bay leaf
3 tablespoons olive oil
½ cup water
8 gingersnap cookies, crushed
2 tablespoons brown sugar, packed
⅓ cup water
3 tablespoons flour

TO MAKE ROAST:

- Prick beef roast thoroughly with fork.
- Place roast in large plastic freezer bag.
- Mix water, red wine vinegar, onion, cloves, peppercorns, salt, and bay leaf; pour into freezer bag.
- Refrigerate two to three days, turning several times.
- Remove beef from marinade; pat dry.
- Strain marinade; reserve liquid.
- Heat oil in Dutch oven until hot.
- Cook beef in hot oil, turning occasionally, until brown, approximately 10 minutes.
- Remove beef; pour off fat.
- Heat 2 cups of the reserved marinade and ½ cup water in a Dutch oven until boiling; reserve remaining marinade.
- Return beef to Dutch oven; reduce heat.
- Cover and simmer until beef is tender, approximately two hours.
- Remove beef to heated platter; keep warm.
- Pour liquid from Dutch oven into large measuring cup; skim fat from liquid.
- Add enough reserved marinade to measure 2½ cups. If liquid measures more than 2½ cups, boil rapidly to reduce to 2½ cups.
- Return to Dutch oven.
- Stir in gingersnap crumbs and brown sugar.
- Mix ⅓ cup water and flour; stir gradually into liquid.
- Heat to boiling, stirring constantly.
- Boil and stir one minute.
- Strain gravy; serve with beef.

Surry Brisket with Chive Sauce

Serves **10**
Preparation time: 35 minutes
Cooking time: 4 hours

**Pair this recipe with
Cardinal Point Vineyard & Winery
Cabernet Sauvignon.**

If you have any leftovers,
they get better every day.

BRISKET
4–6 pounds beef brisket
2 quarts water
4 beef bouillon cubes
2 onions, chopped
5 large carrots, chopped
4 ribs celery, chopped
4 sprigs parsley
4 bay leaves
10 peppercorns
6 whole allspice
1 teaspoon salt
4 links Surry sausage (or substitute smoked sausage)

CHIVE SAUCE
1 tablespoon butter
1 tablespoon shallots, minced
2 tablespoons flour
2 cups beef broth from strained cooking broth
4 tablespoons cream
4 tablespoons fresh chives, minced

TO MAKE BRISKET:
◆ Preheat oven to 500 degrees.
◆ Sear beef brisket in oven for 25 minutes in roasting pan, fat side up.
◆ Turn over and sear for an additional 10 minutes.
◆ Transfer beef brisket to Dutch oven.
◆ Mix pan drippings with 2 quarts hot water and mix in beef bouillon cubes; stir to dissolve beef bouillon cubes.
◆ Pour liquid mixture over beef brisket.
◆ Stir in onions, carrots, celery, parsley, bay leaves, peppercorns, allspice, and salt.
◆ Bring to a boil; reduce heat.
◆ Cover and simmer for two hours or until meat is tender.
◆ Stir in Surry sausage; simmer for an additional one to two hours.
◆ Remove beef and sausage; keep warm.
◆ Strain broth and discard solids; reserve broth.

TO MAKE SAUCE:
◆ Melt butter; stir in shallots and cook until soft.
◆ Blend in flour.
◆ Slowly add beef broth from strained cooking broth.
◆ Simmer broth 10 minutes.
◆ Blend in cream and chives.
◆ Slice meats and pour sauce over meats.

Pungo Pot Roast

Advance preparation required.

Serves 6
Preparation time: 15 minutes
Cooking time: 3 hours

Pair this recipe with Valhalla Vineyards Syrah.

Even the kids will enjoy this dish.

1½ cups dry sherry
½ cup regular or low-sodium soy sauce
½ cup water
2 tablespoons minced garlic
2 teaspoons dry mustard
2 teaspoons dried thyme
½ teaspoon ground ginger
2½–3 pounds boneless chuck roast

TO MAKE ROAST:

◆ Mix sherry, soy sauce, water, garlic, dry mustard, thyme, and ginger in a plastic bag.
◆ Place roast in bag and seal; refrigerator for 24 hours.
◆ Remove roast from marinade, saving marinade.
◆ Sear roast in 5-quart Dutch oven over medium-high heat.
◆ Preheat oven to 325 degrees.
◆ Pour reserved marinade over roast.
◆ If the marinade does not cover the meat, add additional sherry and soy sauce to your taste.
◆ Bring to a boil over high heat on stove.
◆ Cover roast with a tight-fitting lid.
◆ Place in preheated 325 degree oven and cook for three hours.
◆ Remove roast from cooking liquid; strain cooking liquid through a sieve.
◆ The strained liquid can be poured over the cooked meat or thickened depending on your preference.

Dijon-Maple Pork Tenderloin with Apples

Serves 8

Preparation time: 10 minutes
Cooking time: 25 minutes

Pair with Rockbridge Vineyard Riesling.

A wonderful dish when apples are in season. Slice the pork and fan it over the warm apples.

1 package of pork tenderloin (2 pieces per package)
¼ cup Dijon-style mustard
6 tablespoons maple syrup, divided
1 tablespoon fresh rosemary, chopped
½ teaspoon salt
¼ teaspoon pepper
4 Granny Smith apples, peeled and cut into wedges

TO MAKE TENDERLOIN:

◆ Preheat oven to 325 degrees.
◆ Mix Dijon-style mustard, 2 tablespoons maple syrup, rosemary, salt, and pepper to make a sauce.
◆ Cover tenderloin with sauce.
◆ Cook in roasting pan in preheated 325 degree oven for approximately 25–35 minutes, or until internal temperature reaches 160 degrees.
◆ Cook Granny Smith apples in large skillet on high heat until brown.
◆ Stir in remaining 4 tablespoons maple syrup.
◆ Serve with pork.

Mushroom & Blue Cheese Stuffed Pork Chops

Serves 4

Preparation time: 20 minutes
Cooking time: 30—35 minutes

Pair this recipe with North Mountain Vineyard & Winery Vidal Blanc.

A fabulous combination of flavors.

4 pork loin rib chops, cut 1¼ inches thick
2 tablespoons butter
1 cup mushrooms, sliced
2 green onions, finely chopped approximately 4 tablespoons
2 tablespoons chopped pecans or walnuts
4 tablespoons crumbled blue cheese
2 tablespoons apple, orange, or pineapple juice

TO MAKE PORK CHOPS:

◆ Preheat oven to 375 degrees.
◆ Trim fat from pork chops.
◆ Make a pocket in each pork chop by cutting a horizontal slit from the fat side of the chop almost to the bone; set aside.
◆ Melt butter in a small saucepan; cook the mushrooms, green onions, and pecans or walnuts until onions are tender.
◆ Remove from heat; stir in blue cheese.
◆ Spoon one-quarter of vegetable, nut and cheese mixture into each pork chop pocket.
◆ Fasten the pockets with a toothpick, if necessary.
◆ Brush chops with fruit juice.
◆ Bake uncovered in preheated 375 degree oven for 30 minutes or until internal temperature is 160–165 degrees.

Beer Brined Pork Chops

Advance preparation required.

Serves 4
Preparation time: 10 minutes
Cooking time: depends on whether you grill or bake your pork chops

Pair this recipe with St. George Pale Ale or Ingleside Plantation Vineyards Chardonnay.

Brining enhances the flavor and keeps the pork tender.

2 cups water
12 ounces of St. George India Pale Ale
3 tablespoons minced garlic
3 tablespoons kosher salt
2 tablespoons sugar
4 thick boneless pork chops

TO MAKE PORK CHOPS:

- Mix water, St. George India Pale Ale, garlic, salt, and sugar to make brine; stir until sugar and salt are dissolved.
- Pour brine in plastic bag.
- Place pork chops in brine; refrigerate.
- Marinate pork chops not less than 30 minutes and no more than eight hours.
- Prepare grill to medium heat.
- Grill until internal temperature reaches 160 degrees.
- Cover chops with aluminum foil and let stand for 10 minutes before serving.

Autumn Pork Tenderloin

Advance preparation required.

Serves 6
Preparation time: 20 minutes
Cooking time: 20 minutes

Pair this recipe with King Family Vineyards Michael Shaps Viognier.

A simple family dinner. It can be started in the morning and cooked in the evening.

1½ pounds pork tenderloin
½ teaspoon salt or more as needed
2 cups apple juice (or enough to cover the tenderloin in the baking dish)
1 cup apple butter
½ cup brown sugar
4 tablespoons water
1 teaspoon ground cinnamon
½ teaspoon ground cloves

TO MAKE RED PORK TENDERLOIN:

- Prick pork tenderloin all over with a small knife.
- Sprinkle pork with salt; place in a 13 X 9 X 2 baking dish.
- Pour apple juice, to cover, over pork and let stand for at least 30 minutes at room temperature or in the refrigerator for up to several hours.
- Mix apple butter, brown sugar, water, cinnamon, and cloves in a separate bowl; set aside.
- Preheat oven to 350 degrees.
- Drain apple juice from baking dish.
- Bake pork in a preheated 350 degree oven for 10 minutes.
- Remove pork from oven; brush with apple butter mixture.
- Return to oven; and bake for an additional 10 minutes.
- The internal temperature of the pork when done should be between 160—165 degrees; do not overcook.
- Let pork sit for 10 minutes before carving and serving.

Rosemary Crusted Pork Chops with Pears

Serves 6
Preparation time: 15 minutes
Cooking time: 40 minutes

**Pair this recipe with
Chateau Morrisette Pinot Noir.**

For those who prefer a more subtle rosemary
flavor, adjust the amount of rosemary.

4 tablespoons finely chopped fresh rosemary
4 cloves garlic, finely minced
1 teaspoon black pepper
1 teaspoon salt
Olive oil flavored cooking spray
1 large red onion, cut into eighths
6 boneless pork loin chops, ½ inch thick
½ cup dry white wine
3 pears, peeled and quartered
2 teaspoons light brown sugar

TO MAKE PORK CHOPS:

◆ Preheat oven to 200 degrees.
◆ Mix rosemary, garlic, pepper, and salt; set aside.
◆ Spray a large skillet with cooking spray; heat over medium heat.
◆ Stir in onions; cook for five minutes or until lightly browned.
◆ Remove onions from skillet.
◆ Spray each side of pork chops with cooking spray; press rosemary mixture firmly onto each side of pork chops.
◆ Spray each side of pork chops again with cooking spray.
◆ Place pork chops in skillet; cook over medium heat for six minutes per side.
◆ Stir white wine into skillet, cover skillet, and cook for 10 minutes.
◆ Remove pork chops from skillet; place in an ovenproof dish; cover.
◆ Place pork chops in a preheated 200 degree oven to keep warm.
◆ Add cooked onions, pears, and brown sugar to skillet.
◆ Cook for 10 minutes, stirring occasionally.
◆ Spoon pear mixture over pork chops.

Portsmouth Pork Burritos

Serves 2
Preparation time: 30 minutes
Cooking time: 5 minutes

Pair this recipe with North Mountain Vineyard & Winery Riesling.

Thai and Mexican cooking meet Tidewater.

1 pound pork tenderloin, cooked and shredded or finely chopped
2 tablespoons grated fresh gingerroot
1 clove garlic, crushed
1 small onion, diced
2 cups dry coleslaw mix with carrots
1 teaspoon sesame oil
3 tablespoons soy sauce
2 tablespoons lime juice
1 tablespoon honey
2 teaspoons ground coriander
4 large (10-inch) flour tortillas, warmed
Fresh cilantro, chopped (optional)

TO MAKE BURRITOS:

- Heat large nonstick skillet over medium-high heat.
- Stir in gingerroot, garlic, onion, and coleslaw mix; cook until vegetables are wilted.
- Mix sesame oil, soy sauce, lime juice, honey, and ground coriander in a bowl.
- Stir about one minute to completely blend.
- Toss cooked pork with dressing.
- Spoon equal portions of shredded pork and cooked vegetables onto warm tortillas and garnish with cilantro.
- Roll up and serve immediately.

Pork Tenderloin with Williamsburg Porter™ & Cherry Demi-Glace

Advance preparation required.

Serves 4
Preparation time: 10 minutes
Cooking time: 25–35 minutes

Pair this recipe with Williamsburg Porter™.

This recipe is built around fresh, local ingredients, but cherries have a short season in Virginia; the canned ones work great, too. While we're blessed with the fruits of the Bay, we're also lucky to live near the pork capital of the country.

1½–2 pounds fresh Virginia pork tenderloin
1 cup pitted and halved fresh Virginia cherries or 8 ounces canned black cherries
1 cup Williamsburg Porter™
1 cup veal stock or chicken stock
Sprig fresh thyme or pinch (¼ teaspoon) dry thyme
2 bay leaves
1 medium shallot chopped fine
4 tablespoons butter, divided
Fresh chopped parsley
¼ teaspoon each salt and ground black pepper

TO MAKE PORK:

- Marinate pork in beer and cherries overnight in refrigerator.
- Remove pork from marinade and reserve marinade.
- Brown pork on all sides in a heavy skillet over high heat.
- Remove pork to a warm plate; cover with foil.
- Stir 3 tablespoons butter and chopped shallots into skillet; cook until shallots begin to soften, approximately one minute.
- Stir in veal stock, thyme, and bay leaves.
- Deglaze pan (loosen food particles stuck on bottom of pan with a wooden spoon and incorporate into sauce) and cook until volume is reduced to one-third of the original volume.
- Place pork back in skillet, add salt and pepper, and cover skillet.
- Reduce heat to medium; simmer over medium heat approximately 10–15 minutes or until internal temperature reaches 160 degrees.
- Remove pork to serving plate to rest; cover with foil.
- Pour reserved beer and cherry marinade into skillet and stir; reduce marinade over high heat until the sauce coats the back of a spoon evenly, about two to three minutes.
- Remove pan from heat and stir in remaining 1 tablespoon butter.
- Slice pork tenderloin, place on serving platter, and pour Williamsburg Porter™ and cherry demi-glace on top.
- Garnish with chopped parsley and serve.

- *Prep Tip:* To pit fresh cherries, roll fruit firmly between thumb and index and middle fingers to loosen pit; insert tip of paring knife into top of fruit and pop out pit. (Brewer's note: If you have children who like fresh cherries, it is physically impossible to do this faster than they can eat them.)

from Old House Vineyards:

Pork Loin with Roasted Red Pepper Gravy

Advance preparation required.

Serves 6
Preparation time: 30 minutes
Cooking time: 45–75 minutes

Pair this recipe with Old House Vineyards Merlot.

A garlicky spiced-rubbed pork loin with a gravy made with pureed roasted red peppers.

ROASTED RED PEPPER SAUCE
3 red bell peppers
Olive oil

GRAVY
2 tablespoons olive oil
1½ cups chopped onions
1 tablespoon garlic
¼ teaspoon ground red pepper
1½ cups beef stock
1 cup water

PORK LOIN
Pork loin roast, approximately 3 pounds
Chopped garlic
Olive oil

TO MAKE RED PEPPER SAUCE:
◆ Slice three red bell peppers; place on a broiler pan.
◆ Rub peppers with olive oil to coat; place peppers under broiler and blacken skins, approximately 5–10 minutes, turning as each side blackens.
◆ Remove from oven, let cool, and remove skins; set aside.

TO MAKE GRAVY:
◆ Pour oil into heavy skillet over medium heat; add onions; cook until onions are browned.
◆ Stir in roasted red peppers, garlic, and ground red pepper.
◆ Stir in beef stock and water; mix and bring to a boil.
◆ Reduce heat; simmer for 90 minutes.
◆ Purée liquid mixture in a blender or food processor; keep warm.
◆ Preheat oven to 450 degrees.

TO MAKE PORK LOIN:
◆ Make incisions in pork loin roast; rub roast with mixture of garlic and olive oil; rub into incisions.
◆ Roast pork roast for 10 minutes.
◆ Reduce oven temperature to 250 degrees.
◆ Roast until internal temperature reaches 150–155 degrees, approximately 45–75 minutes.
◆ Remove from oven; cover pork roast loosely with foil; let stand for 15 minutes.
◆ Slice roast and serve with gravy.

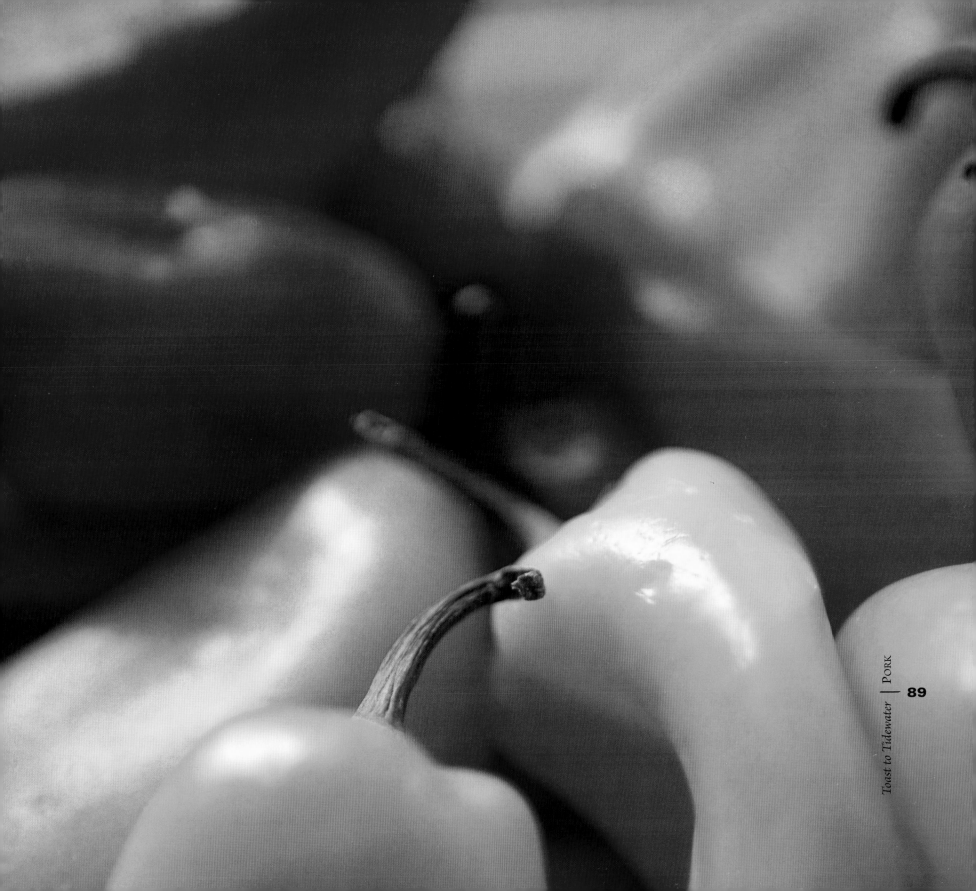

Peanut Chicken

Serves 8

Preparation time: 25 minutes
Cooking time: 4 minutes per piece of chicken

Pair this recipe with Breaux Vineyards Barrel-Fermented Chardonnay.

2 eggs, beaten
½ cup milk
1 cup flour
2 cups finely chopped salted peanuts without skins
1 teaspoon salt
1 teaspoon pepper
8 skinless boneless chicken breasts, approximately ½ inch thick
Peanut oil

TO MAKE CHICKEN:

- Combine eggs and milk in a pie pan; mix well.
- Combine flour, crushed peanuts, salt, and pepper in a shallow bowl; mix well.
- Place chicken in egg mixture, then dredge in flour mixture.
- Pour ½ inch of peanut oil in skillet; heat over medium high.
- Preheat oven to 250 degrees.
- Place chicken in peanut oil; cook approximately two minutes per side or until tender and golden brown.
- Remove chicken from oil; place on a paper towel-lined baking sheet.
- Keep chicken warm in preheated 250 degree oven until ready to serve.

Honey & Orange Chicken

Serves 4

Preparation time: 20 minutes
Cooking time: 55 minutes

Pair this recipe with Wintergreen Winery Riesling.

A great dish to take to a friend in need of a helping hand.

4 chicken breasts with bones and skin
1 tablespoon sunflower oil
4 green onions, chopped
1 clove garlic, crushed
3 tablespoons honey
4 tablespoons orange juice
1 orange, peeled and segmented
2 tablespoons soy sauce

TO MAKE CHICKEN:

- Preheat oven to 375 degrees.
- Place chicken breasts in a single layer in baking dish.
- Heat sunflower oil in a small saucepan.
- Gently cook green onions and garlic until softened but not brown, approximately two minutes.
- Stir in honey, orange juice, orange segments, and soy sauce; cook until honey has completely dissolved.
- Pour sauce over chicken.
- Bake in preheated 375 degree oven for 55 minutes or until chicken is cooked.
- Baste with sauce every 15 minutes during cooking.

Chicken Jubilee

Serves 4
Preparation time: 30 minutes
Cooking time: 25 minutes

Pair this recipe with Chateau Morrisette or Stone Mountain Vineyards Chardonnay.

The lemon cream sauce and the chicken can be prepared in advance and cooked before serving.

CHICKEN
4 boneless, skinless chicken breasts, weighing approximately 6 ounces each
1 cup chopped sun-dried tomatoes in oil, drained and 2 tablespoons oil reserved
Pepper to taste
4 ounces crumbled Feta cheese

LEMON CREAM SAUCE
2 tablespoons butter
2 tablespoons flour
1 cup milk
¼ cup coarsely chopped onion
1 chicken bouillon cube, crumbled
1 lemon, juice and zest

TO MAKE CHICKEN:
◆ Preheat oven to 350 degrees.
◆ Spray a baking pan with nonstick spray and set aside.
◆ Place chicken between two sheets of plastic wrap.
◆ Flatten chicken with mallet or rolling pin.
◆ Brush chicken with reserved sun-dried tomato oil and season with pepper.
◆ Mix Feta cheese and tomatoes.
◆ Spread one-quarter of cheese mixture on one side of each piece of chicken.
◆ Fold chicken to enclose cheese mixture.
◆ Use toothpick to hold chicken together, if necessary.
◆ If not cooking the chicken immediately, cover and refrigerate for up to four hours.
◆ Bring chicken back to room temperature before placing in oven.
◆ Place chicken in baking pan; bake in a preheated 350 degree oven for approximately 25 minutes until lightly browned and cooked through.
◆ To serve, slice the chicken on an angle and fan over rice.
◆ Garnish with Lemon Cream Sauce and serve immediately.

TO MAKE SAUCE:
◆ Melt butter in a saucepan over medium-low heat.
◆ Stir in flour until well blended.
◆ Stir in the cream and onion; cook, stirring with wire whisk, until thick and smooth.
◆ Stir in bouillon cube, juice, and zest from lemon.
◆ Stir to blend; pour sauce through a fine mesh strainer.
◆ Pour sauce over chicken and serve.

Pecan-Crusted Chicken with Mango Salsa

Advance preparation required.

Serves 4
Preparation time: 30 minutes
Cooking time: 30 minutes

Pair this recipe with Oakencroft Vineyard & Winery NV Sweet Virginia.

A wonderful party dish
that can be made in advance.

SALSA
2 ripe mangos
1 fresh jalapeno pepper, seeded and chopped
1 large clove garlic, minced
½ cup chopped red onion
¼ cup chopped cilantro
3 kiwis, peeled and chopped

CHICKEN
2 cups pecans
½ cup plain yogurt
Hot pepper sauce to taste
Salt to taste
4 boneless and skinless chicken breasts halves, very cold

TO MAKE SALSA:

◆ Peel mangos.
◆ Cut mango by slicing diagonally from outside of fruit toward the seed.
◆ Cut mango slices into ¼ inch cubes; place in medium bowl.
◆ Stir in jalapeno pepper, garlic, red onion, and cilantro and mix gently.
◆ Stir in kiwis; gently mix.
◆ Make at least six hours before serving and chill, covered, in refrigerator.

TO MAKE CHICKEN:

◆ Chop pecans in food processor until very fine, but not pulverized.
◆ Place yogurt in medium-size bowl.
◆ Stir in hot pepper sauce; mix.
◆ If not cooking the chicken immediately, the yogurt mixture may be placed in refrigerator for up to eight hours.
◆ Preheat oven to 400 degrees.
◆ Spray baking sheet three times with cooking spray.
◆ Roll chicken in yogurt mixture and then in pecans.
◆ Place on baking sheet.
◆ Place baking sheet on bottom shelf of oven and bake in preheated 400 degree oven for 30 minutes, turning chicken every 10 minutes.
◆ Remove chicken from oven; top with salsa.

Since 1968, the Hampton Jazz Festival has brought the best of jazz, rhythm and blues, and blues to the Tidewater area. The festival is always held during the last full weekend in June. Typically, artists are announced and tickets go on sale in early April. The wide variety of featured performers has included current artists Anita Baker, India.Arie, and Mary J. Blige; musical icons Gladys Knight, Herbie Hancock, Patti LaBelle, and Stevie Ray Vaughan; and legends Count Basie, Dizzy Gillespie, Duke Ellington, and B.B. King. The three-day festival is held at Hampton Coliseum, an architecturally distinct venue featuring dramatic metallic vapor exterior lighting and excellent interior acoustics.

Thai Coconut Chicken

Serves 4
Preparation time: 30 minutes
Cooking time: 20 minutes

Pair this recipe with Rockbridge Vineyard White Riesling.

A quick but elegant meal.

½ cup crushed peanuts
1 small onion, chopped
1 clove of garlic, crushed
1 teaspoon grated lemon peel
1 tablespoon sugar
1 teaspoon salt
1 teaspoon cayenne pepper
4 chicken breasts, weighing approximately 6 ounces each
Olive oil
15 ounces cream of coconut
Soy sauce to taste
Jasmine rice

TO MAKE CHICKEN:

- Mix peanuts, onion, garlic, lemon peel, sugar, salt, and cayenne pepper.
- Coat chicken with peanut mixture.
- Heat olive oil in a skillet over medium-high heat.
- Cook coated chicken three minutes per side in skillet.
- Stir in cream of coconut and soy sauce to taste; cook 10 minutes on low heat or until done.
- Serve over cooked jasmine rice.

Balsamic Chicken with Mushrooms

Serves 4
Preparation time: 20 minutes
Cooking time: 20–30 minutes

Pair this recipe with First Colony Winery Cabernet Franc.

Good as an entrée or over a salad.

2 teaspoons vegetable oil, divided
6 tablespoons balsamic vinegar, divided
4 teaspoons Dijon-style mustard
½ teaspoon dried thyme leaves, divided
2 large cloves garlic, crushed
4 skinless chicken breasts weighing approximately 4 ounces each and approximately ¼ inch thick
2 cups small mushrooms, halved
⅓ cup chicken broth

TO MAKE CHICKEN:

- Heat 1 teaspoon of vegetable oil in a large nonstick skillet.
- Mix 4 tablespoons of balsamic vinegar, Dijon-style mustard, ¼ teaspoon thyme, and garlic in a medium bowl.
- Stir in chicken and coat with liquid mixture.
- Transfer the chicken and liquid mixture to the skillet.
- Cook the chicken in the liquid until cooked, approximately seven minutes per side.
- Transfer the chicken to a platter; keep warm.

Continued on next page...

continued from page 94:

TO MAKE CHICKEN:

- Stir the remaining oil, balsamic vinegar, chicken broth, and remaining thyme into the skillet; heat.
- Stir in mushrooms; cook stirring occasionally until the mushrooms are a deep brown, approximately two minutes.
- Simmer until mixture has thickened.
- Serve chicken topped with mushrooms.

Chicken in White Hall Vineyards Wine

Serves 6
Preparation time: 25 minutes
Cooking time: 30 minutes

Pair this recipe with White Hall Vineyards Cabernet Sauvignon.

¼ cup chopped fresh parsley
1 tablespoon chopped fresh rosemary
2 teaspoons chopped fresh sage
2 cloves garlic, finely chopped
¾ teaspoon salt
¼ teaspoon black pepper
12 boneless, skinless chicken thighs, approximately 2½ pounds
6 thin slices ham, cut in half
1 tablespoon olive oil
1 cup White Hall Vineyards Cabernet Sauvignon

TO MAKE CHICKEN:

- Mix parsley, rosemary, sage, garlic, salt, and pepper in a small bowl.
- Lay a chicken thigh skin side down on a clean work surface.
- Spoon 1 teaspoon of the herb mixture onto each piece of chicken and spread out to cover chicken.
- Place one piece of ham over herb mixture.
- Roll up chicken; tie with string.
- Heat olive oil in a large skillet over high heat; add chicken bundles and cook.
- Turn chicken frequently, until well browned, approximately six minutes.
- Add White Hall Vineyards Cabernet Sauvignon; reduce to medium-low heat.
- Simmer, turning occasionally, until chicken is cooked through and wine has been reduced to a glaze, approximately 20 minutes.
- Remove string from chicken and serve.

Chicken in Phyllo with Shrimp, Feta & Olives

Serves 4
Preparation time: 25 minutes
Cooking time: 40 minutes

Pair this recipe with Horton Cellars Winery Spotswood Trail Chardonnay.

An elegant dinner entrée
to serve guests.

6 sheets phyllo pastry
1 cup butter, melted
4 boneless skinless chicken breast halves, approximately 4 ounces each
Salt and pepper to taste
½ cup ranch salad dressing
8 large shrimp, peeled, deveined and cut in half horizontally
⅓ cup pitted and chopped Calamata olives
¼ cup chopped green onions
4 tablespoons Feta cheese, crumbled
Finely chopped parsley as garnish

TO MAKE CHICKEN:

- Preheat oven to 350 degrees.
- Cover phyllo sheets with a damp towel until ready to use; this keeps it from drying out and breaking.
- Place one sheet of phyllo on flat surface and brush with butter; repeat process for remaining sheets of phyllo, stacking one sheet on top of another after brushing with butter.
- Cut phyllo into four 6 X 8 rectangles.
- Coat one side of chicken breast with ranch dressing.
- Place chicken, dressing side down, on the diagonal on top right corner of prepared phyllo.
- Place shrimp, olives, green onions, and Feta cheese on top of chicken.
- Fold corner of phyllo sheet over chicken.
- Fold over sides and carefully roll up chicken and pastry into a package.
- Place phyllo seam side down on lightly oiled baking sheet.
- Brush phyllo tops with butter.
- Bake in preheated 350 degree oven for 40 minutes or until browned.
- Garnish with chopped parsley.

Chicken Curry

Serves 4
Preparation time: 20 minutes
Cooking time: 20 minutes

Pair this recipe with White Hall Vineyards Gewurztraminer or North Mountain Vineyard & Winery Chambourcin.

The traditional toppings for curry are called "boys" and should be served in odd number quantities. We recommend peanuts, coconut, raisins, bacon, chutney, green onions, and hard-cooked egg.

1 tablespoon vegetable oil
4 tablespoons flour
1 tablespoon curry powder
1 teaspoon ground cumin
¼ teaspoon salt
4 thin, skinless chicken breasts weighing approximately 4 ounces each
1 cup orange juice
1 cup chicken broth
2 tablespoons mango chutney
½ cup sour cream
2 tablespoons chopped cilantro

TO MAKE CHICKEN:

- Heat oil in a large nonstick skillet.
- Mix flour, curry powder, cumin, and salt in plastic bag.
- Place chicken in bag and shake to coat with flour mixture.
- Remove chicken from plastic bag, shake off excess coating; reserve remaining flour.
- Transfer chicken to skillet; cook approximately three minutes per side, making sure chicken is cooked all the way through.
- Transfer chicken to a platter and keep warm.
- Stir excess flour into skillet and mix with pan juices.
- Gradually add orange juice and broth, stirring constantly and scraping up the browned bits from the bottom of the skillet.
- Stir in chutney.
- Bring to a boil and cook; stirring constantly until mixture thickens, approximately one minute.
- Stir in sour cream until blended.
- Simmer 30 seconds.
- Spoon sauce over chicken and sprinkle with cilantro.
- Serve over rice.

Sizzling Noodles

Serves **6**
Preparation time: 45 minutes
Cooking time: 10–15 minutes

**Pair this recipe with
Farfelu Vineyards Riesling.**

This dish can be served hot or cold.

FISH SAUCE
Make sauce before cooking chicken.
  4 tablespoons fish sauce
  4 tablespoons fresh lime or lemon juice
  4 tablespoons tomato puree
  4 tablespoons sugar
  1 teaspoon dried chilies or to taste

ENTRÉE
  ½ cup vegetable oil
  4 cloves garlic, crushed
  1 pound boneless and skinless chicken, cut into bite-size pieces
  14 ounces soft tofu, drained well and cut into bite-size chunks
  8 shrimp, peeled and deveined
  4 eggs
  8 ounces Thai rice noodles, soaked in cold water for four hours or
    soaked in warm water for 30 minutes
  ½ cup ground peanuts
  2 cups fresh bean sprouts
  Green onion cut lengthwise into 2-inch pieces
  Chopped cilantro, lemon or lime wedges for garnish

TO MAKE SAUCE:

◆ Mix fish sauce, fresh lime or lemon, tomato puree, sugar, and dried chilies; set sauce aside.

TO MAKE ENTRÉE:

◆ Heat vegetable oil in a medium wok; brown the garlic.
◆ Stir in chicken, tofu, and shrimp; brown for a few minutes, stirring constantly.
◆ Stir in eggs; cook until eggs are soft.
◆ Drain rice noodles.
◆ Turn heat up to high.
◆ Stir rice noodles into wok.
◆ Stir in sauce; cook for three minutes, stirring constantly.
◆ Stir in the peanuts, bean sprouts, and green onion; cook for two minutes.
◆ Garnish with chopped cilantro and lemon or lime wedges.

Totally Different Fried Turkey

Advance preparation required.

Serves 15
Preparation time: 20 minutes
Cooking time: 3 ½ minutes per pound of turkey or until internal temperature reaches 165 degrees in the leg joint, not in solid meat. This cooking time is for an oil temperature between 340–350 degrees.

Pair this recipe with King Family Vineyards Michael Shaps Viognier.

A totally different taste that everyone will rave about.

15 pounds or less fresh whole turkey
¼ cup kosher salt
4 heads of garlic, separated but not peeled
6 bay leaves
1 cup peeled and chopped fresh gingerroot
2 teaspoons red pepper flakes
2 cups soy sauce
5 to 6 quarts water
¼ cup sugar
Large container for brine
Peanut oil
Turkey fryer

TO MAKE TURKEY:

◆ Mix kosher salt, garlic, bay leaves, fresh ginger, red pepper, soy sauce, water, and sugar in a very large pot to make a brine.
◆ Bring brine to a boil.
◆ Remove brine from the heat; cool completely.
◆ The brine can and should be made a day in advance.
◆ Remove neck and giblets from the turkey.
◆ Submerse turkey into cold brine.
◆ Place brine in refrigerator, covered, for no more than eight hours.
◆ Remove turkey from brine and dry the skin and cavities.
◆ Discard brine.
◆ If not cooking the turkey immediately, cover with aluminum foil (completely and tightly) and return to refrigerator for no more than six hours.
◆ Cook turkey in peanut oil as directed by your turkey fryer instructions.

Don't Be Crabby, Another Year Younger Menu

(Birthdays)

◆

Naked Mountain's Smoked Salmon Mousse

Portside Garlic Portobello Caps

Pair with White Hall Vineyards Merlot or

Chateau Morrisette Winery Merlot

◆

Buckroe Beach Soft Shells

Asparagus Delights

Pair with Villa Appalaccia Winery Pinot Grigio

◆

Zuppa Inglese—serve in balloon wine glasses

and add birthday candles

Pair with Barboursville Vineyards Brut or

Kluge Estate Winery and Vineyard Kluge Estate SP

Another year younger?
Oh, how could it be?
You're just another day wiser,
So smile with glee!
May your heart be filled with love,
your days filled with joy,
For you're another year younger,
and many more to be!

—*Toast written by Barrett Bussard, JLNVB member*

Section photograph underwritten by:
Farm Fresh Supermarkets

In late May, the City of Chesapeake toots its own horn for three fun-filled days. Honoring the city's anniversary, the Chesapeake Jubilee is a good-time celebration that began in 1983. The Jubilee brings together its citizens and neighbors from surrounding communities for mouth-watering food, carnival rides, and games, plus wholesome entertainment that can be enjoyed by every family member.

Over the years, the Jubilee has become Chesapeake's biggest yearly event. The annual Kiwanis Shrimp Fest kicks off the celebration, and the ever-popular Jam Preserves Contest is a must-see. In addition, the 4-H activities and live stage performances by local and national musical artists always attract record number crowds. All this merriment takes place in the Chesapeake City Park.

Cape Henry Crab

Serves **6**
Preparation time: 25 minutes
Cooking time: 15 minutes

**Pair this recipe with
Rapidan River Vineyards Dry Riesling.**

This is the dinner to make when you want to impress your guests.

1 pound lump crabmeat
2 slices bacon, cooked, drained, and crumbled
1 cup evaporated skim milk
1 teaspoon chicken bouillon granules
2 tablespoons cornstarch
1 teaspoon dry mustard
½ teaspoon paprika
½ teaspoon celery salt
½ cup chili sauce
1 teaspoon tarragon vinegar
½ cup low-fat mayonnaise
1 teaspoon capers
Hot pepper sauce
½ cup dry sherry
8 ounces aged Gouda cheese, shredded

TO MAKE CRAB:

◆ Spray ½ cup individual baking dishes with nonstick cooking spray.

◆ Check crabmeat; remove any cartilage or shell.

◆ Place crab in large bowl; mix in bacon.

◆ Pour milk into a saucepan; dissolve bouillon granules and cornstarch in milk; stir over low heat until thick.

◆ Remove from heat; stir in dry mustard, paprika, celery salt, chili sauce, tarragon vinegar, mayonnaise, capers, and hot pepper sauce to taste.

◆ Mix sauce with crabmeat; stir in dry sherry.

◆ Preheat oven to 350 degrees.

◆ Divide crab mixture evenly between prepared baking dishes; top with Gouda cheese.

◆ Bake in preheated 350 degree oven for 15 minutes or until hot and golden brown.

◆ Can be frozen, defrosted, and cooked.

Buckroe Beach Soft Shell Crabs

Advance preparation required.

Serves 6
Preparation time: 15 minutes
Cooking time: 16–24 minutes

Pair this recipe with Villa Appalaccia Winery Pinot Grigio.

The soft shell crabs can be prepared fresh or frozen, if not in season.

12 soft shell crabs, cleaned
12 ounces St. George Porter
2–3 eggs, beaten
2 cups Panko crumbs or white cornmeal
1 teaspoon dry mustard
1 teaspoon paprika
1 teaspoon garlic powder
Vegetable oil

TO MAKE CRABS:

◆ Soak soft shell crabs in beer for 15 minutes.
◆ Turn soft shell crabs and continue soaking for an additional 15 minutes.
◆ Place eggs in a shallow pan.
◆ Mix Panko crumbs, dry mustard, paprika, and garlic powder in a shallow bowl.
◆ Dip soft shell crabs into egg mixture and then dredge in Panko crumbs.
◆ Pour ½ inch of vegetable oil into a cast iron skillet; heat over moderate heat.
◆ Preheat oven to 250 degrees.
◆ Fry three soft shell crabs at a time for approximately two to three minutes per side.
◆ Line a cookie sheet with a paper towel.
◆ Place cooked soft shell crabs on cookie sheet and place in preheated 250 degree oven to keep warm as you cook the other soft shell crabs.

If you are looking for an incredibly scenic drive on a beautiful afternoon, look no further! The Colonial Parkway is 23 miles of beautifully engineered landscape that combines the region's natural and cultural resources into a memorial roadway of the American colonial experience. The Parkway connects Jamestown, Williamsburg, and Yorktown, an area often referred to as the "historic triangle." These are three of the most historically significant sites in English North America and represent the beginning and end of English colonial America.

The Colonial Parkway also includes Green Spring, the seventeenth century plantation home of Virginia's colonial governor, Sir William Berkeley, and the Cape Henry Memorial, which marks the approximate site of the first landing of the Jamestown colonists in April 1607.

Along your drive you will enjoy viewing a variety of natural resources, including extensive wetlands, forest, fields, shorelines, streams, and beautiful water birds, as well as rare, threatened, and endangered plants and animals. So jump in the car and enjoy the sights around you as you drive through history.

Colonial Crab Risotto with Ham & Cheese

Advance preparation required.

Serves 6
Preparation time: 45 minutes
Cooking time: 20 minutes

Pair this recipe with Horton Cellars Winery Spotswood Trail Chardonnay.

Can be served as an entrée or a first course.

RISOTTO

- 1 teaspoon saffron, crumbled
- 6 cups chicken stock
- 4 tablespoons butter
- 1 cup chopped onion
- 2½ cups Arborio rice
- ½ cup white wine
- 4 ounces Virginia Gouda cheese, shredded
- ½ cup backfin crabmeat
- ½ pound shredded country cured Smithfield or Surry ham
- Yellow cornmeal
- Olive oil
- Spinach leaves for garnish

CREAM SAUCE

- 1 cup white wine
- ¼ cup chopped green onions
- ½ cup heavy cream

TO MAKE RISOTTO:

- ◆ Stir saffron into chicken stock; let sit for one hour to flavor stock.
- ◆ Bring chicken stock to a simmer and keep hot.
- ◆ Melt butter in a 3-quart saucepan; stir in onions and cook until soft.
- ◆ Stir in rice and coat all the grains; stir in wine and let the rice absorb the wine.
- ◆ Slowly add ½ cup hot chicken stock into the rice, stirring constantly.
- ◆ When chicken stock is absorbed into the rice, add more chicken stock and continue until all the chicken stock is absorbed into the rice, and the rice is al dente.
- ◆ Remove from heat; stir in Gouda cheese; mix well.
- ◆ Stir in crabmeat and ham.
- ◆ Pat rice and crab mixture into 15 X 10 baking pan.
- ◆ Smooth out mixture, cover with plastic wrap, and refrigerate for several hours.
- ◆ Remove from refrigerator, cut rice-crab mixture into 3-inch rounds with a cookie cutter.
- ◆ Coat rounds with cornmeal, shake to remove excess cornmeal.
- ◆ Pour olive oil into a nonstick skillet and cook rounds over medium-high heat until golden brown.
- ◆ Place cooked rounds on fresh spinach leaves and serve with a raspberry vinaigrette or cream sauce.

TO MAKE CREAM SAUCE:

- ◆ Place white wine and green onion in a small saucepan.
- ◆ Bring to a boil; keep at boiling point, until the sauce is reduced by half.
- ◆ Strain out onions, return liquid to saucepan, add cream, and simmer until thickened, approximately 5–10 minutes.

Wine & Cheese Shrimp with Caramelized Onions

Serves 6
Preparation time: 50 minutes
Cooking time: 40 minutes

Pair this recipe with Loudoun Valley Vineyards Vinifera White or Oakencroft Vineyard & Winery VC Classic.

A wonderfully rich dish.

1½ pounds thinly sliced yellow onion
1 teaspoon sugar
4 roma tomatoes
4 tablespoons fresh basil, cut into thin strips
1 pound large (21–29 count) shrimp, cooked and peeled
4 tablespoons butter
4 tablespoons flour
1 cup milk
¼ cup Chardonnay
½ teaspoon kosher salt
¼ teaspoon white pepper
3 ounces sharp Cheddar cheese, shredded
6 ounces Gruyére cheese, shredded
1 cup fresh bread crumbs

TO MAKE SHRIMP:

◆ Spray nonstick skillet with cooking spray.
◆ Place sliced onions in skillet and cover; cook over low heat until soft, stirring occasionally.
◆ Sprinkle sugar over onions.
◆ Continue cooking onions covered over low heat, stirring occasionally until golden brown and caramelized, approximately 20 minutes.
◆ Preheat oven to 350 degrees.
◆ Coat 8 X 8 baking dish with nonstick cooking spray.
◆ Cover bottom of baking dish with caramelized onions.
◆ Cut tomatoes in half; scoop out and discard seeds and pulp.
◆ Dice tomatoes and scatter over the onions.
◆ Sprinkle basil over tomatoes.
◆ Place cooked shrimp on top of basil and tomatoes.
◆ Melt butter in medium saucepan over medium-low heat.
◆ Stir in flour; cook over low heat for 60 seconds.
◆ Slowly add milk, allowing the milk to be absorbed into the flour mixture forming a roux.
◆ When all the milk has been absorbed, slowly add wine.
◆ Stir in salt and white pepper.
◆ Add Cheddar cheese and melt.
◆ Pour sauce over shrimp.
◆ Sprinkle Gruyére cheese over sauce; top with bread crumbs.
◆ Bake in preheated 350 degree oven for 40 minutes or until the bread crumbs are brown and sauce is bubbling.
◆ Cover dish with aluminum foil; let sit for 5-10 minutes before serving.
◆ Serve with brown rice and a salad.

Margarita Shrimp

Advance preparation required.

Serves **6**
Preparation time: 15 minutes
Cooking time: 5 minutes

Pair this recipe with Valhalla Vineyards Chardonnay.

If you substitute ½ cup coconut milk for ½ cup heavy cream, you get pina colada shrimp!

1½ pounds large raw shrimp, peeled and deveined
4 tablespoons lime juice, divided
Salt and white pepper to taste
2 ripe avocados
3 tablespoons olive oil
2 tablespoons finely chopped shallots
⅓ cup tequila
2 tablespoons Grand Marnier® liqueur
1 cup heavy cream
3 tablespoons chopped red bell pepper

TO MAKE SHRIMP:

◆ Mix shrimp, 3 tablespoons lime juice, salt, and white pepper in a bowl; toss to coat shrimp.
◆ Let stand for 45 minutes.
◆ Peel the avocados and remove the pits; cut into ½-inch slices lengthwise.
◆ Place avocados in a small bowl; add remaining 1 tablespoon lime juice.
◆ Mix gently to coat avocado slices.
◆ Heat olive oil in a large frying pan over medium heat; stir in shrimp and marinade; cook, stirring for approximately two minutes.
◆ Sprinkle shallots over shrimp; cook for 10 seconds.
◆ Remove from heat; stir in tequila, Grand Marnier®, heavy cream, salt, pepper, and chopped red peppers.
◆ Mix briefly, and stir in avocado slices; return to heat, and cook for one minute.
◆ Transfer the shrimp and avocado to plates.
◆ Bring the sauce to a full boil for 45 seconds.
◆ Spoon sauce over shrimp and avocado.
◆ Serve with rice.

from St. George's Brewery:
Drunken Shrimp Overboard

Advance preparation required.

Serves 6
Preparation time: 20 minutes
Cooking time: 40–60 seconds

Pair this recipe with St. George Porter or Golden Ale.

If you are not able to grill, reserve marinade and sauté shrimp over medium-high heat on the stove until pink.

12 ounces St. George Porter
1/3 cup toasted sesame oil
1 tablespoon frozen lime juice concentrate
2 tablespoons Thai fish sauce
5 cloves garlic, crushed
1 teaspoon powdered cardamom
1 teaspoon Chinese red chili paste
1 1/2 pounds large shrimp (30 count), heads off but in shell
Wooden skewers soaked in water for several hours

TO MAKE SHRIMP:

- Mix St. George Porter, sesame oil, lime juice, fish sauce, garlic, cardamom, and chili paste; pour into a large plastic bag.
- Place shrimp in plastic bag; marinate overnight in refrigerator.
- Prepare a hot grill.
- Place shrimp on soaked bamboo skewers, three per skewer.
- Grill about 40–60 seconds per side or until shells just turn orange-pink; do not over cook.
- Serve immediately.

Landside Lime-Seasoned Grilled Salmon

Advance preparation required.

Serves 4
Preparation time: 10 minutes
Cooking time: 12 minutes

**Pair this recipe with
Lake Anna Winery Lake Side White
or Horton Cellars Winery Petit Manseng.**

Add lime slices for added color—this is a wonderful option for lunch.

1/4 cup vegetable oil
1/4 cup lime juice
1 tablespoon water
1 tablespoon soy sauce
2 teaspoons sesame oil
2 teaspoons honey
4 fresh salmon, tuna, or sea bass steaks, cut 1 inch thick, weighing approximately 1 pound
1 cup shredded mixed greens or spinach
Lime slices

TO MAKE SALMON:

- Mix vegetable oil, lime juice, water, soy sauce, sesame oil, and honey.
- Place fish in plastic bag; pour vegetable oil mixture over fish.
- Marinate in refrigerator for 30–60 minutes, turning occasionally.
- Place mixed greens on large platter or four individual plates.
- Grease grill rack.
- Drain fish, reserving marinade.
- Grill fish on an uncovered grill directly over medium-hot coals for 8–12 minutes or until fish flakes easily; turn over fish halfway through cooking.
- Transfer reserved marinade to small saucepan; heat until bubbly.
- Pour hot marinade over greens; toss to wilt slightly.
- Place grilled fish on top of greens.

Virginia Beach Beer-Boiled Shrimp

Serves 12
Preparation time: 30 minutes
Cooking time: 53 minutes

**Pair this recipe with
St. George Pilsner.**

A quick and easy way to entertain
a large group of people.

4½ gallons water
6 cans (12 ounces each) beer
2 large lemons
3 tablespoons Old Bay™ seasoning
4 bay leaves
4 ribs celery
2–3 pounds corned beef with seasoning package
3 pounds small red potatoes
6 ears of corn, shucked and cut in half or thirds
2 pounds kielbasa (smoked sausage)
4 pounds shrimp (21 count)

TO MAKE SHRIMP:

◆ You need a powerful propane burner like the kind you use for a fried turkey.
◆ Fill 32-quart pot with water and beer.
◆ Slice lemons in half and squeeze lemon juice into pot of water and beer.
◆ Place lemons in the pot.
◆ Place Old Bay™ seasoning, bay leaves, and celery in pot.
◆ Place corned beef in pot with seasonings and bring to a boil over low heat, covered.
◆ Simmer for 30 minutes.
◆ Bring water to a rolling boil; you do not want to lose the boil when you add remaining ingredients.
◆ Place potatoes in pot and boil for 10 minutes.
◆ Drop in corn and boil for an additional five minutes.
◆ Drop in sausage and boil an additional five minutes.
◆ Add shrimp; stir and watch closely as the shrimp will cook in two to three minutes—do not overcook the shrimp.
◆ Drain the pot; serve in big bowls on tables and enjoy.
◆ Drawn butter, cocktail sauce, regular butter, and mustard are nice additions.

Hampton Bay Sparkling Scallops

Serves 6
Preparation time: 10 minutes
Cooking time: 20–25 minutes

**Pair this recipe with
Prince Michel Vineyards
Virginia Brut Sparkling Wine.**

For a sophisticated dinner, this is a great first course. Not too overpowering for the palate.

2 cups Champagne (brut or extra dry) or white wine
2 tablespoons shallots, finely chopped
4 sprigs fresh thyme
2 pounds sea scallops
2 tablespoons flour
4 tablespoons sour cream
1 tablespoon Dijon-style mustard
Salt and freshly ground pepper to taste
4 tablespoons fresh bread crumbs

TO MAKE SCALLOPS:

◆ Mix Champagne, shallots, and thyme in a large saucepan; bring to a boil over high heat.

◆ Reduce heat to medium; simmer until liquid is reduced in volume by half.

◆ Remove sprigs of thyme.

◆ Stir in scallops and continue to cook over medium heat for five to seven minutes, until the contents of the pan almost reach a boil and the scallops have become firm and white; scallops should be underdone at this point.

◆ Remove scallops with a slotted spoon and place in an ovenproof au gratin dish.

◆ Mix flour, sour cream, and Dijon-style mustard thoroughly in a separate bowl.

◆ Stir flour mixture into remaining liquid in the pan; mix in completely.

◆ Bring to boil over high heat until it is the consistency of heavy cream; this may take two to five minutes depending on how much liquid the scallops released.

◆ Salt and pepper to taste.

◆ Spoon the liquid over the scallops and sprinkle with bread crumbs.

◆ Place under a preheated broiler until bread crumbs have browned, approximately two to four minutes.

◆ Serve immediately.

Nearly half a million people will visit Hampton Bay Days, one of the largest family-oriented festivals on the East Coast. The three-day festival held in September in downtown Hampton highlights the beauty and importance of the Chesapeake Bay.

The festival features headline musical entertainers on several stages, bay activities, and educational exhibits, as well as Saturday night fireworks and a juried indoor art show. Along with arts and crafts, sport and water events, a car show, and a carnival, there is an abundance of culinary delights featuring the Chesapeake Bay's scrumptious seafood. This festival has something every family member will enjoy.

Pistachio-Encrusted Grouper from Wintergreen Winery

Serves 4
Preparation time: 10 minutes
Cooking time: 4–5 minutes

Pair this recipe with Wintergreen Winery Black Rock Chardonnay Reserve.

Not a grouper fan?
Try this with your favorite fish.

½ cup ground pistachio nuts
3 tablespoons butter, melted
2 tablespoons unflavored dry bread crumbs
1 teaspoon chopped fresh basil
½ teaspoon minced garlic
⅛ teaspoon salt
Pinch freshly ground pepper
1 tablespoon oil for jelly roll pan
4 skinless grouper fillets or snapper, cod, or sea bass
Salt and pepper to taste
⅓ cup flour
2 tablespoons grapeseed oil or vegetable oil
Spinach leaves
Lemon wedges

TO MAKE GROUPER:

◆ Mix pistachios, butter, bread crumbs, basil, garlic, salt, and pinch of pepper in small bowl; set aside.
◆ Preheat broiler.
◆ Lightly oil a 15 X 10 X 1 jelly roll pan.
◆ Season fish fillets with salt and pepper.
◆ Place flour on a sheet of waxed paper.
◆ Dip each side of fish fillets in flour, shaking off excess.
◆ Heat oil in large nonstick skillet over high heat.
◆ Place fish in skillet and cook until golden brown on both sides, approximately three minutes; the fish should not be cooked through.
◆ Transfer to baking pan; spread fish evenly with pistachio mixture.
◆ Broil five inches from heat for four to five minutes until browned and cooked through.
◆ Cover loosely with foil if topping browns too quickly.
◆ Arrange fish on steamed spinach leaves with lemon wedges.

Bayside Balsamic-Glazed Salmon

1 pound fresh salmon fillets
Vegetable cooking spray
½ cup balsamic vinegar
2 tablespoons Dijon-style mustard
Salt and pepper to taste

Serves 4
Preparation time: 20 minutes
Cooking time: 15 minutes

**Pair this recipe with
First Colony Winery Cabernet Franc.**

An easy but flavorful way to prepare salmon.

TO MAKE SALMON:

◆ Rinse salmon; pat dry.
◆ Heat nonstick skillet; spray with vegetable cooking spray.
◆ Cook salmon on flesh side for five minutes on medium heat; turn salmon and cook on skin side for three minutes.
◆ Remove salmon; place on plate.
◆ Stir balsamic vinegar into skillet; cook on medium heat until balsamic vinegar has reduced by half, approximately three minutes.
◆ Lower heat.
◆ Stir in Dijon-style mustard; mix into a smooth glaze.
◆ Salt and pepper salmon; return salmon skin side down to skillet.
◆ Cover skillet; cook skin side down for two minutes.
◆ Remaining glaze may be spooned over salmon.

Unicorn Winery's Pecan-Crusted Catfish

½ cup coarse plain bread crumbs
½ cup ground pecans
1½ tablespoons butter, melted
1 teaspoon fresh lemon juice
Salt
Fresh ground pepper
2 catfish fillets, weighing approximately 12 ounces each

Serves 6
Preparation time: 20 minutes
Cooking time: 15–30 minutes

Pair this recipe with Unicorn Winery Seyval.

This dish is best served with a salad of light greens and batter bread.

TO MAKE CATFISH:

◆ Mix bread crumbs and ground pecans.
◆ Mix melted butter and lemon juice in a small bowl.
◆ Gently toss bread crumb and pecan mixture into butter-lemon mixture, just enough to coat crumbs—do not saturate the bread crumbs.
◆ Mix in salt and pepper to taste.
◆ Preheat oven to 350 degrees.
◆ Wash catfish fillets and pat dry with a clean towel.
◆ Place catfish fillets in a greased 10 X 8 glass baking dish.
◆ Spread bread crumb mixture over catfish fillets approximately ⅛-inch thick pressing by hand or with a rubber spatula.
◆ Bake in preheated 350 degree oven for 15–30 minutes or until fish is done and topping is golden brown.

Stonewall Vineyards' Flounder Vidal

Serves 4

Preparation time: 10 minutes
Cooking time: 10–15 minutes

**Pair this with
Stonewall Vineyards & Winery Vidal Blanc.**

Serving with wedges
of lemon adds a nice touch.

1½ pounds flounder fillets
Freshly ground pepper
Dijon-style mustard
2 tablespoons olive oil
½ cup Stonewall Vineyards & Winery Vidal Blanc wine
1 lemon

TO MAKE FLOUNDER:

◆ Rinse and dry flounder fillets.
◆ Pepper both sides of flounder fillets.
◆ Lightly coat both sides with Dijon-style mustard.
◆ Heat skillet over low heat; add oil and lightly brown fillets.
◆ Pour in wine, cover, and simmer three to five minutes, depending on thickness.

Baked Chesapeake Oysters D'Italia

Serves 4

Preparation time: 20 minutes
Cooking time: 20 minutes

**Pair this recipe with Valhalla Vineyards
Sangiovese.**

Most oyster lovers prefer them on the half shell
or steamed. Here is a way for even more people
to enjoy oysters.

4 ounces spaghetti noodles
Olive oil
1 pint oysters
2 cups rustic red sauce (*see page 64*)
Garlic salt
Pepper
4 ounces Parmesan cheese, shredded
3 ounces shredded mozzarella cheese

TO MAKE OYSTERS:

◆ Break spaghetti into small pieces.
◆ Boil spaghetti in salted water with a touch of olive oil until tender; drain.
◆ Place oysters in their own liquor in a saucepan and heat to just below boiling; cook for two minutes.
◆ Drain oysters and reserve ½ cup oyster liquor.
◆ Preheat oven to 350 degrees.
◆ Spread ¾ cup rustic red sauce on the bottom of 12 X 8 baking dish.
◆ Place half of cooked spaghetti noodles in a layer over sauce.
◆ Place all of the oysters over spaghetti noodles.
◆ Sprinkle with garlic salt, pepper, and ½ cup Parmesan cheese.
◆ Top with remaining spaghetti noodles.
◆ Mix reserved ½ cup oyster liquor with the remaining sauce.
◆ Pour mixture over the top of the spaghetti noodles.
◆ Sprinkle top of the sauce with remaining Parmesan cheese and shredded mozzarella cheese.
◆ Bake in preheated 350 degree oven for 20 minutes or until cheese is thoroughly melted.

Crusted Sea Bass with Shrimp & Roasted Tomato Butter Sauce

Serves 6
Preparation time: 20 minutes
Cooking time: 40 minutes

**Pair this recipe with
Cardinal Point Vineyard & Winery A6.**

You can substitute your favorite fish fillet or chicken breast pounded to ¼-inch thickness.

1 pint ripe grape tomatoes
2 medium cloves garlic, minced
4 tablespoons olive oil, divided
Salt and freshly ground pepper
6 sea bass fillets, weighing approximately 6 ounces each
½ teaspoon chili powder
½ teaspoon cumin
1 tablespoon butter
1½ pounds large uncooked shrimp, peeled and deveined
1 cup dry white wine
6 ounces fresh spinach leaves, torn into strips
Juice of 2 lemons, approximately ¼ cup
4 tablespoons butter

TO MAKE SEA BASS:

◆ Preheat oven to 400 degrees.
◆ Place tomatoes into a shallow baking pan; sprinkle with minced garlic.
◆ Drizzle tomatoes and garlic with 1 tablespoon olive oil.
◆ Season with salt and pepper.
◆ Roast tomatoes in preheated 400 degree oven for 15–20 minutes.
◆ Season sea bass fillets with salt and pepper.
◆ Stir chili powder and cumin into 2 tablespoons olive oil.
◆ Brush one side of sea bass fillets with chili powder mixture.
◆ Heat butter and remaining 1 tablespoon olive oil in large skillet over medium-high heat.
◆ Place sea bass fillets seasoned side down in the skillet; cook for four minutes.
◆ Turn sea bass fillets over and cook for an additional four minutes.
◆ Remove sea bass fillets to a platter and keep warm.
◆ Stir shrimp into the pan and season with salt and pepper; cook until just opaque, approximately five minutes.
◆ Remove shrimp to a bowl.
◆ Stir wine into the pan.
◆ Stir in spinach and lemon juice; cook until just reduced, approximately five minutes.
◆ Stir in roasted tomatoes and shrimp; reduce the heat to low, add butter, and stir until melted.
◆ To serve, place a sea bass fillet in the center of a dinner plate. Spoon tomato and shrimp mixture around sea bass fillets. Drizzle sauce over spinach leaves and over sea bass fillets.

Atlantic Blackened Redfish

Serves **6**
Preparation time: 15 minutes
Cooking time: 10 minutes

**Pair this recipe with
King Family Vineyards Chardonnay
or Kluge Estate Winery & Vineyard
New World Red.**

Loaded with zesty flavor.

8 tablespoons butter
1 tablespoon paprika
2½ teaspoons salt
1 teaspoon onion powder
1 teaspoon garlic powder
1 teaspoon cayenne pepper
¾ teaspoon white ground pepper
¼ teaspoon black pepper
½ teaspoon dried thyme
½ teaspoon dried oregano
6 redfish or snapper fillets, cut about ½ inch thick and weighing approximately 8 ounces each

TO MAKE RED FISH OR SNAPPER:

◆ Heat large cast iron skillet over very high heat until beyond smoking stage (at least 10 minutes); you should be able to see white ash in bottom.
◆ Melt butter in a separate pan; lower heat and keep butter warm.
◆ Heat serving plate in 250 degree oven.
◆ Mix paprika, salt, onion powder, garlic powder, cayenne pepper, white pepper, black pepper, thyme, and oregano in a small bowl.
◆ Dip each fish fillet in melted butter to coat both sides.
◆ Sprinkle fish fillets evenly and generously with spice mixture; pat in spice by hand.
◆ Place fish fillets in hot skillet; cook for four to five minutes per side.
◆ Place cooked fish fillets on warmed serving plate in preheated oven while cooking remaining fish fillets.

Southern Gentleman Ginger Tuna

Advance preparation required.

Serves 4
Preparation time: 15 minutes
Cooking time: 8–9 minutes

**Pair this recipe with
Rapidan River Vineyards Gewurztraminer.**

For added presentation,
garnish this dish with green onions,
cherry tomatoes, and lime wedges.

4 tuna steaks, sashimi grade
1 cup soy sauce
½ cup olive oil
1 cup dry sherry
4 cloves garlic, finely chopped
4 tablespoons fresh ginger, finely chopped
4 tablespoons grated orange zest
Green onions, cherry tomatoes, or lime wedges for garnish

TO MAKE TUNA:

- Place tuna steaks in a shallow dish.
- Mix soy sauce, olive oil, dry sherry, garlic, ginger, and orange zest; pour over tuna steaks.
- Marinate for one hour, turning tuna steaks at least twice.
- Remove tuna steaks, reserving marinade, and place on oiled rack in broiler pan.
- Set broiler rack four inches from heat.
- Broil tuna steaks for three to four minutes, then turn over tuna steaks and broil until done, approximately three more minutes.
- Transfer tuna steaks to platter.
- Boil reserved marinade on stovetop for two minutes; either pour sauce over fish to serve or place remaining sauce in gravy boat.

Surfside Smoked Salmon Fettuccini

Serves 6
Preparation time: 30 minutes
Cooking time: 20 minutes

**Pair this recipe with Stone Mountain Vineyards
or King Family Vineyards Chardonnay.**

For an elegant taste, sprinkle caviar over the top
of this dish.

1 onion, chopped
6 cloves garlic, chopped
2 tablespoons olive oil
2 teaspoons fresh tarragon, chopped
8 ounces sliced smoked salmon
1 cup dry sherry
2 tablespoons flour
1½ cups light cream
12 ounces fettuccini, cooked and drained
1 tablespoon caviar, optional

TO MAKE SALMON:

- Cook onion and garlic in olive oil over low heat until soft, approximately 10 minutes.
- Stir in tarragon, salmon, and dry sherry; bring to a boil.
- Reduce heat; simmer until liquid is reduced in volume by half, approximately five minutes.
- Mix flour and cream together; add to pan slowly; simmer over low heat until warm.
- Serve over warm fettuccini.

Mariner Mussels in Cider & Cream

Serves 4
Preparation time: 15 minutes
Cooking time: 20–25 minutes

**Pair this recipe with
Breaux Vineyards Seyval Blanc.**

Be sure to serve this one
with crusty French bread.

2 pounds fresh mussels, cleaned and de-bearded
1½ tablespoons butter, divided
3 shallots, finely chopped
2 cups hard cider, divided
1 sprig fresh thyme
1 bay leaf
1 cup heavy cream
Salt and pepper, to taste
1 tablespoon snipped chives

TO MAKE MUSSELS:

◆ Throw away any broken or opened mussels.
◆ Melt ¾ tablespoon butter in large pan.
◆ Stir in shallots; cook gently for two minutes.
◆ Mix in 1½ cups hard cider, thyme, and bay leaf.
◆ Simmer until liquid mixture is reduced in volume by one-third, approximately 10 minutes.
◆ Stir heavy cream and mussels into reduced mixture.
◆ Cook for three to five minutes, or until mussels have opened, shaking pan every few minutes.
◆ Remove mussels to a bowl leaving juices in skillet.
◆ Simmer juices until reduced by half.
◆ To the reduced juice, stir in remaining ¾ tablespoon butter, ½ cup hard cider, salt, pepper, and chives.
◆ Heat gently.
◆ Pour two-thirds of sauce over mussels and serve the remainder in a dish for dipping sauce.

Cuckold Creek Oysters

Serves 6
Preparation time: 30 minutes
Cooking time: 10 minutes

**Pair this recipe with
Ingleside Plantation Vineyards Pinot Gris.**

6 puff pastry shells
8 tablespoons butter, divided
1 shallot, peeled and minced
1 pound mushrooms, sliced
2 jars (4 ounces each) sliced red pimento peppers, drained
5 tablespoons flour
1 quart shucked, raw oysters in their liquor
1 cup heavy cream
1 tablespoon Worcestershire sauce
2 tablespoons dry sherry
Fresh parsley for garnish

TO MAKE OYSTERS:

- Cook puff pastry shells according to directions on package; keep warm.
- Melt 3 tablespoons butter in a large skillet; add shallots to pan and cook until translucent.
- Stir mushrooms into shallots; cook over medium-low heat for five minutes or until they begin to brown.
- Add pimentos to mushrooms and cook for an additional five minutes.
- Remove the pan from the heat and set aside.
- Preheat oven to 150 degrees.
- Melt the remaining 5 tablespoons of butter slowly in a Dutch oven and slowly stir flour into the butter with a wooden spoon to make a roux.
- Stir butter-flour mixture, leaving no lumps in mixture, and set aside.
- Poach oysters in their liquor in a separate skillet; remove oysters from liquid when the edges of the oyster begin to curl.
- Strain contents of skillet through a strainer into a bowl large enough to hold the oyster liquor; set liquor aside.
- Remove oysters from strainer and place in a separate bowl, cover tightly with aluminum foil, and keep warm in a preheated 150 degree oven.
- Reheat roux over medium-low heat.
- Add approximately 1 cup of oyster liquor gradually to the roux, stirring with a wooden spoon.
- Cook roux until the mixture becomes thick and smooth; add heavy cream slowly to roux and blend well.
- Add Worcestershire sauce and dry sherry to cream mixture; cook for several minutes.
- Taste and adjust seasoning and dry sherry to taste.
- Drain accumulated liquid from oysters and vegetables.
- Return oysters and vegetable mixture to the sauce and heat thoroughly.
- Place mixture in puff pastry shells, garnish with parsley, and serve at once.

Give a Cheer Menu

(Sports events, tailgating, etc.)

◆

Fabulous Pesto-Feta Spread
Pair with Wintergreen Winery Black Rock Chardonnay Reserve

◆

Tortellini Chicken Salad or Virginia Tailgate Panini
Eggplant Stuffed Peppers
Rosemary Roasted Green Beans
Red Potato Salad with Garlic Dressing
Pair with Rockbridge Vineyard DeChiel Pinot Noir

◆

Coconut Macaroons and Beach Balls
Pair with Wintergreen Winery Raspberry or
Chateau Morrisette Frosty Dog

Vegetables & Side Dishes

Section photograph dedicated to:
Our Expert Wine Panel

Our team is going to win
Hip, hip hooray!
Oh, how it is going to be
a grand ol' day!
For your team,
Give us a cheer.
Because when they win,
We all want to hear!

—*Toast written by Barrett Bussard, JLNVB member*

NEWPORT NEWS
A City By Any Other Name

What kind of a name is Newport News? Visitors to the Hampton Roads area often question the meaning of this odd-sounding city name. The history dates back to the settling of America. Christopher Newport, captain of the Susan Constant, led a three-ship fleet carrying Jamestown settlers to the New World in 1607.

Captain Newport made several subsequent trips to England and returned to the new settlements. When the original settlers abandoned Jamestown after the Starving Time of 1610, they encountered Captain Newport where the James River meets the Chesapeake Bay. Newport encouraged their return by spreading information that reinforcements of men and supplies had arrived. The location where Newport and the settlers met became known for "Newport's good news," eventually evolving into this unique and charming city name, Newport News.

Eggplant Stuffed Peppers

Serves 4
Preparation time: 40 minutes
Cooking time: 45–50 minutes

Boiling water

4 red or green bell peppers, cut in half lengthwise, deseeded, pith removed

4 tablespoons oil

2 large eggplant, peeled and cut into bite-size pieces

3 cloves garlic, minced

1 cup Italian flavored bread crumbs

1/2 cup fresh basil, finely chopped

2 ounces Parmesan cheese, grated

Pepper to taste

1/2 cup fresh parsley

8 ounces flavored goat cheese, sliced into 8 slices

Marinara sauce

1/2 cup pine nuts, toasted

4 large fresh basil leaves, cut into thin strips

TO MAKE PEPPERS:

- Place bell peppers in boiling water for two minutes to soften; drain thoroughly.
- Pour oil into a nonstick skillet, stir in eggplant and garlic, and cook until eggplant is very soft, approximately 30 minutes.
- Remove from heat.
- Preheat oven to 350 degrees.
- Stir bread crumbs into eggplant mixture; toss until bread crumbs are moistened.
- Stir in basil, Parmesan cheese, pepper, and fresh parsley.
- Fill softened bell peppers halfway with eggplant mixture.
- Place a slice of goat cheese over eggplant mixture and cover with more of the eggplant mixture, enough to fill the pepper.
- Place peppers in an 8 X 8 baking pan with 1/2 cup water.
- Bake in preheated 350 degree oven for 45-50 minutes.
- Top with warm marinara sauce, toasted pine nuts, and fresh basil.

Stir-Fried Eggplant with Garlic Sauce

Serves 4
Preparation time: 20 minutes
Cooking time: 7 minutes

1 cup low-sodium chicken broth, cold
1 teaspoon cornstarch
¼ cup vegetable oil
1 tablespoon oriental sesame oil
1 tablespoon minced garlic
1 large red jalapeno chili, seeded, thinly sliced
1 pound Japanese eggplant, trimmed, cut lengthwise into quarters
¼ cup thinly sliced fresh basil
Ground white pepper and salt to taste

TO MAKE EGGPLANT:

◆ Mix cold chicken broth with cornstarch in small bowl until smooth.

◆ Heat vegetable oil and sesame oil in wok or heavy large skillet over high heat.

◆ Stir in garlic and jalapeno chili; cook until garlic sizzles approximately 10 seconds.

◆ Stir in Japanese eggplant; stir fry until tender and golden approximately five minutes.

◆ Stir in basil, stirring for one minute.

◆ Stir broth mixture into the eggplant; boil until sauce thickens and coats eggplant, approximately one minute.

◆ Season to taste with ground white pepper and salt.

◆ Serve hot with rice on the side.

The Great Dismal Swamp is a geological wonder. For millions of years before the swamp was formed, it was under the sea. Today, it is viewed by naturalists and other scientists as one of the best outdoor laboratories in the world.

Before the days of refrigeration, water from the swamp was put in kegs and would stay fresh for a long time. People spoke of the magical qualities of the swamp's tea-colored water and how, if it was regularly consumed, it would prevent illness and promote a longer life.

Just who discovered the Great Dismal Swamp and when is unknown, but William Byrd II visited the swamp in 1728 while surveying the boundary line between Virginia and North Carolina. Today, the Great Dismal Swamp National Wildlife Refuge is a wonderful place to surround yourself in the solitude of greenery and cypress.

Oasis Winery's Mushroom Risotto

Serves 4–6
Preparation time: 15 minutes
Cooking time: 25-30 minutes

1 tablespoon olive oil
3 tablespoons butter, divided
3 teaspoons garlic, divided
¾ pound mushrooms (shiitakes, oyster, morels), chopped
1 cup chopped onion
2 cups Arborio rice
½ cup Oasis Winery Chardonnay
2 cups chicken stock, hot
4 ounces Parmesan cheese, grated

TO MAKE RISOTTO:

◆ Melt olive oil and 2 tablespoons butter in large heavy saucepan; stir in 1 teaspoon garlic and cook over low heat until soft.
◆ Stir in mushrooms and cook until soft; set aside.
◆ Melt remaining 1 tablespoon butter in a separate pot over medium heat.
◆ Stir in remaining 2 teaspoons garlic and the onion; cook until soft.
◆ Stir in Arborio rice; stir until rice is coated with butter mixture.
◆ Stir in Oasis Winery Chardonnay; cook for five minutes, stirring constantly.
◆ Add ½ cup hot stock at a time to rice stirring until completely absorbed into rice before stirring in more stock.
◆ Stir in mushrooms.
◆ Stir in Parmesan cheese.
◆ Serve immediately.

Portside Garlic Portobello Caps

Advance preparation required.

Serves 6
Preparation time: 20 minutes
Cooking time: 8–10 minutes

Leftover cream cheese can be frozen
for later use.

6 portobello mushroom caps, weighing approximately 2 ounces each
2 cups dry red wine
¼ cup balsamic vinegar
¼ cup olive oil
1 tablespoon fresh thyme
6 ounces cream cheese, softened
2½ ounces Parmesan cheese, grated
¼ teaspoon kosher salt
¼ teaspoon Worcestershire sauce
¼ teaspoon black pepper
½ teaspoon hot pepper sauce
2 teaspoons garlic powder
1 teaspoon dried parsley

TO MAKE MUSHROOMS:

- Clean portobello mushrooms, if necessary, and remove the stems.
- Mix dry red wine, balsamic vinegar, olive oil, and thyme in a glass bowl.
- Wipe cap side of portobello mushroom with wine mixture; place cap side down in a glass baking dish.
- Pour remaining wine mixture directly over the gills of the portobello mushrooms.
- Cover and marinate in refrigerator for 30 minutes or up to two hours.
- While portobello mushrooms are marinating, complete the following:
- Cream together cream cheese, Parmesan cheese, kosher salt, Worcestershire sauce, black pepper, hot pepper sauce, garlic powder, and parsley.
- This mixture needs to be at room temperature for proper spreading consistency.
- Remove portobello mushrooms from the marinade when ready to serve.
- Grill over high heat for approximately four minutes a side or until tender.
- When the portobello mushrooms are tender, spread cream cheese mixture over the gill side of the mushroom.
- Close the cover of the grill, allowing the cream cheese mixture to melt.
- Serve immediately.
- If you want to grill the portobello mushrooms ahead of time, remove from grill before adding cheese mixture and refrigerate covered until ready to serve.
- Bring the portobello mushrooms and cream cheese mixture to room temperature when ready to serve.
- Preheat oven to 350 degrees.
- Spread cream cheese mixture over the gill side of portobello mushrooms and place in preheated 350 degree oven for approximately 10 minutes or until hot and bubbly.

Asiago Chive Mashed Potatoes

Serves **8**
Preparation time: 25 minutes

12 medium unpeeled red potatoes cut in half, approximately 3 pounds
8 tablespoons butter, softened
16 ounces sour cream
4 ounces Asiago cheese, shredded
1 teaspoon salt
1 teaspoon pepper
2 tablespoons chopped chives
1 teaspoon garlic powder
4 tablespoons chopped green onions

TO MAKE POTATOES:

◆ Place potatoes in a large pot; cover with cold water.
◆ Bring water to a boil; cook until potatoes are tender, approximately 20 minutes.
◆ Drain water.
◆ Mash potatoes in a deep bowl; add butter; blend until smooth.
◆ Add sour cream; blend until smooth.
◆ Add Asiago cheese, salt, pepper, chives, garlic powder, and green onions; blend evenly.

Roasted Potato & Fennel Hash

Serves **8**

Preparation time: 30 minutes
Cooking time: 45 minutes for potatoes,
15 minutes for fennel

**An eye-appealing side dish
that goes nicely with pork.**

2 pounds small unpeeled red potatoes, sliced ½ inch thick
1 tablespoon olive oil
Salt and pepper to taste
3 tablespoons butter
3 medium fennel bulbs, trimmed, cored, thinly sliced crosswise
1 tablespoon finely chopped fresh thyme
2 tablespoons coarsely chopped fresh parsley

TO MAKE HASH:

◆ Preheat oven to 425 degrees.
◆ Spread red potato slices in a single layer on two lightly oiled baking sheets.
◆ Drizzle the olive oil over the red potato slices; season with salt and pepper.
◆ Roast red potato slices for approximately 45 minutes, turning occasionally until browned and crisp.
◆ Melt butter in a large skillet; stir in sliced fennel.
◆ Cook fennel over moderate heat, stirring often, until tender, approximately 15 minutes.
◆ Stir in fresh thyme.
◆ Add red potato slices and parsley to the fennel just before serving; stir quickly over high heat until warmed.
◆ Season with salt and pepper.

Cranberry Basmati Rice

Serves 4
Preparation time: 15 minutes
Cooking time: 30 minutes

For taste variation, leave out the onions and add more cranberries. A refreshing twist to rice.

1 teaspoon vegetable oil
1 medium onion, chopped
1½ cups chicken broth
1 cup basmati rice
½ cup orange juice
⅓ cup dried cranberries
1 teaspoon dried orange peel
1 teaspoon salt
¼ teaspoon dried sage
¼ teaspoon black pepper

TO MAKE RICE:

◆ Heat the oil in a large saucepan.
◆ Stir in onion and cook, stirring as need until softened, approximately five minutes.
◆ Stir in chicken broth, rice, orange juice, cranberries, orange peel, salt, sage, and pepper.
◆ Bring broth to a boil; do not stir as this will make rice gummy.
◆ Reduce heat; simmer covered until most of the liquid is absorbed, approximately 15 minutes.
◆ Remove from the heat; let stand 10 minutes or until all the liquid is absorbed.
◆ Fluff with a fork and serve.

Virginia Peanuts & Okra

Serves 4
Preparation time: 15 minutes
Cooking time: 4–5 minutes

¾ cup all-purpose baking mix
¼ cup crushed club style crackers
¾ cup finely chopped dry roasted salted Virginia peanuts, divided
½ teaspoon salt
½ teaspoon pepper
1 pound fresh okra, cut into ¼-inch pieces
Peanut oil

TO MAKE OKRA:

◆ Mix baking mix, crushed crackers, ½ cup chopped peanuts, salt, and pepper in a large bowl.
◆ Stir in okra, coating each piece with mixture and pushing peanut mixture into each piece of okra.
◆ Pour 2 inches of peanut oil into deep skillet; heat to 375 degrees.
◆ Fry approximately ¼ pound of okra at a time for four to five minutes or until golden brown.
◆ Drain cooked pieces on a paper towel.
◆ Place cooked and drained okra in a serving bowl; sprinkle with remaining ¼ cup chopped peanuts.

Marinated Asparagus

Advance preparation required.

Serves **12**
Preparation time: 15 minutes
Cooking time: 4 minutes

This is a nice summertime dish for luncheons or dinner parties.

3 pounds fresh asparagus
2 cans (14 ounces each) hearts of palm, drained and cut into ½-inch-round slices
1 cup olive oil
½ cup balsamic vinegar
3 cloves garlic, crushed
1½ teaspoons salt
1 teaspoon pepper
Cherry tomatoes

TO MAKE ASPARAGUS:

◆ Steam asparagus over boiling water for four minutes.
◆ Remove asparagus and immediately place in ice water for five minutes or until cool.
◆ Drain asparagus well.
◆ Mix cooked asparagus and hearts of palm in a plastic bag.
◆ Mix olive oil, balsamic vinegar, garlic, salt, and pepper in a jar; cover tightly and shake.
◆ Pour dressing over asparagus and hearts of palm in plastic bag.
◆ Seal bag and marinate in refrigerator for eight hours, turning occasionally.
◆ Add cherry tomatoes before serving.

Lemon Carrots with Dill

Serves 6

Preparation time: 20 minutes
Cooking time: 15 minutes

A zesty alternative to liven up a staple vegetable.

½ small onion, minced
1½ pounds carrots, peeled, thinly sliced
4 tablespoons butter, divided
½ cup water
½ teaspoon salt
1 teaspoon sugar
1 tablespoon lemon juice
1 teaspoon dill
Pinch white pepper

TO MAKE CARROTS:

◆ Cook onion and carrots in 2 tablespoons butter until onions are translucent, approximately five minutes.
◆ Stir in water and salt; simmer 10 minutes.
◆ Drain liquid; set carrots aside.
◆ Melt remaining butter in small saucepan; stir in sugar, lemon juice, dill, and white pepper.
◆ Toss carrots in butter mixture.
◆ Heat thoroughly and serve.

Roasted Butternut Squash & Shallots

Serves 8

Preparation time: 20 minutes
Cooking time: 20 minutes

3 cups peeled butternut squash, cut into 1 inch cubes
¼ cup dark brown sugar
1½ tablespoons olive oil
1 teaspoon salt
½ teaspoon black pepper
8 shallots minced
1 tablespoon chopped fresh sage

TO MAKE SQUASH:

◆ Preheat oven to 475 degrees.
◆ Mix butternut squash, brown sugar, olive oil, salt, pepper, and shallots.
◆ Place mixture in a 15 X 10 X 1 baking dish.
◆ Toss well.
◆ Bake in preheated 475 degree oven for 15-20 minutes or until tender; stir occasionally.
◆ Stir in sage after vegetables are finished cooking.

Rosemary Roasted Green Beans

Serves 4

Preparation time: 10 minutes
Cooking time: 20 minutes

This is a great recipe to prepare ahead and refrigerate.

½ pound fresh green beans, washed and cut in half
1 clove garlic, chopped fine
2 small shallots, chopped fine
½ teaspoon salt
½ teaspoon dried rosemary, crushed
½ teaspoon dried thyme, crushed
Olive oil pan spray

TO MAKE GREEN BEANS:

◆ Preheat oven to 425 degrees.
◆ Lightly spray baking sheet with nonstick cooking spray.
◆ Place green beans, garlic, and shallots on baking sheet.
◆ Sprinkle salt, rosemary, and thyme over green beans.
◆ Mist green beans with olive oil spray to lightly coat.
◆ Roast green beans, uncovered, for 10 minutes in 425 degree oven.
◆ Stir green beans and roast for an additional 10 minutes.
◆ The green beans should appear to be shriveled.
◆ This is great prepared ahead and refrigerated.
◆ Reheat for five minutes in 450 degree oven or serve at room temperature.

Ghent Fresh Green Beans

Serves 6
Preparation time: 30 minutes
Cooking time: 10 minutes

Subtle flavor makes these
the most delightful beans in the area.

1½ pounds green beans
5 tablespoons butter, divided
1 heaping teaspoon chopped shallots
¼ teaspoon minced garlic
Pinch of sugar
¼ teaspoon fresh tarragon or marjoram, chopped
Salt and freshly ground black pepper to taste

TO MAKE GREEN BEANS:

◆ Trim the ends of green beans; wash thoroughly.
◆ Melt 4 tablespoons butter in a heavy skillet over medium heat, stirring constantly.
◆ Increase the heat and continue stirring as the butter foams and begins to turn golden brown.
◆ Immediately remove the butter from the heat and carefully pour into a heat-proof container; set aside.
◆ Bring 6-quart pot of salted water to a rolling boil.
◆ Drop in green beans and cook until tender to the bite, approximately six minutes.
◆ Drain green beans; immediately plunge green beans into a bowl of ice water for two to five minutes.
◆ Drain green beans; dry well.
◆ Melt remaining 1 tablespoon butter in a 10-inch skillet over medium heat; cover entire skillet with butter.
◆ When butter begins to brown, add green beans and cook for 90 seconds over high heat.
◆ Constantly toss green beans to prevent burning.
◆ Stir in shallots and garlic and cook for an additional minute, continuing to move green beans around the pan.
◆ Stir in sugar, tarragon or marjoram, salt, and pepper; stir for 10 seconds.
◆ Pour brown butter over green beans; stir once and remove from the heat.

Gabriele Rausse's Red Wine Risotto

Serves 4
Preparation time: 15 minutes
Cooking time: 25–30 minutes

Purchase this wine directly from the winery (see source guide) or use another Virginia Cabernet Sauvignon.

1½ tablespoons butter
1½ tablespoons olive oil
1 small onion, chopped
1¼ cups Arborio rice
1 cup Gabriele Rausse Cabernet Sauvignon, room temperature
2 cups chicken stock, heated
⅛ cup cream
Parmesan cheese, to taste

TO MAKE RISOTTO:

◆ Melt butter in a heavy saucepan; stir in olive oil.
◆ Stir in onions; cook until soft and golden, approximately three minutes.
◆ Mix in rice; stir with wooden spoon approximately one minute.
◆ Make sure all the rice is coated with the butter and olive oil mixture.
◆ Stir Gabriele Rausse Cabernet Sauvignon into rice ½ cup at a time.
◆ Stir constantly with wooden spoon until wine is absorbed into the rice.
◆ Maintain chicken stock at a simmer.
◆ Simmer rice mixture; slowly add ½ cup chicken broth until all broth has been added to rice; stir constantly with wooden spoon in a circular motion from the middle to the outside of the pan.
◆ When all the stock has been absorbed and the rice is al dente, remove from heat.
◆ Stir in cream; mix well.
◆ Garnish with Parmesan cheese.

Steamed Broccoli with Tangy Sauce

Serves 4

Preparation time: 15 minutes
Cooking time: 5–7 minutes

An easy and wonderful blend of flavors.

2 tablespoons soy sauce
2 tablespoons lemon juice
1 teaspoon minced garlic
One head of broccoli

TO MAKE BROCCOLI:

◆ Mix soy sauce, lemon juice, and garlic in small bowl; set aside.
◆ Steam broccoli.
◆ Remove broccoli from steamer; pour sauce over broccoli.

---

from Barboursville Vineyards: White Wine Spinach

Serves 8

Preparation time: 15 minutes
Cooking time: 3–5 minutes

2 tablespoons olive oil
3 tablespoons fresh chopped garlic
3 pounds spinach, stems removed, washed and chopped into 2-inch pieces
¼ cup dry white wine
Salt and pepper to taste

TO MAKE SPINACH:

◆ Heat large skillet on high heat; add olive oil.
◆ Stir in garlic and spinach; cook for one minute.
◆ Stir in dry white wine, salt, and pepper to taste.
◆ Cook for one minute.
◆ Serve immediately.

---

from La Provencale Cellars: Le Mousseux Sorbet

Advance preparation required.

Serves 2

Preparation time: 10 minutes

This also works nicely as a dessert when served with a crisp sugar cookie.

1 cup Le Mousseux Virginia Sparkling Cider
¼ cup granulated sugar

TO MAKE SORBET:

◆ Mix cider and sugar in a deep bowl.
◆ Whisk briskly until sugar is dissolved.
◆ Pour liquid into shallow tray.
◆ Place in freezer until mixture is thoroughly chilled and solid to the touch.
◆ Spoon into wine glasses and serve as a palate refresher between courses.

Founded in 1930 as a division of the College of William and Mary, Old Dominion University has grown significantly since its modest beginnings. Old Dominion's 188-acre campus is located in Norfolk, Virginia, in an area stretching from the Elizabeth River to the Lafayette River. The university prides itself on offering a small-college look and feel in a metropolitan setting.

Old Dominion's mission takes its cue from its Hampton Roads location. Since the early seventeenth century, Hampton Roads has had a significant role in the nation's commerce and industry, in recreation and culture, and in national security. The polycentric urban area is home to extensive scientific and technological activities in marine science, aerospace, ship design and construction, and other industries. Thus, the university places an emphasis on commerce and on international affairs. It also has a significant commitment in science, engineering, and technology. Additionally, as a metropolitan institution, Old Dominion places emphasis on urban issues, including education and health care, and on fine and performing arts.

With an enrollment exceeding 20,000, the university offers 66 undergraduate degree programs and numerous programs at the master's and doctoral levels. Extensive research is performed at the university, with total research grants and contracts valued at more than $50 million annually. Business and research initiatives contribute more the $600 million annually to the economy, making Old Dominion the largest generator of new jobs in the region.

Sweet Potato Stuffed Apples

Serves 5

Preparation time: 40 minutes
Cooking time: 45 minutes

Replace your holiday sweet potato dish with this fragrant, eye-catching delight.

5 large cooking apples
3 tablespoons slivered almonds, divided
2 cups cooked sweet potatoes, mashed
3 tablespoons brown sugar
3 tablespoons maple syrup
1 tablespoon butter, melted
½ teaspoon ground cinnamon
¼ teaspoon salt

TO MAKE STUFFED APPLES:

- Core apples, starting at stem end, without cutting through opposite end; discard core.
- Scoop out pulp to enlarge opening to 2 inches.
- Chop pulp and set aside.
- Preheat oven to 350 degrees.
- Place each apple shell on a 7-inch square of aluminum foil.
- Stir together chopped apple, 2 tablespoons almonds, sweet potatoes, brown sugar, maple syrup, butter, cinnamon, and salt.
- Spoon evenly into apple shells.
- Top with remaining almonds.
- Pull foil up around sides of apples and place in a lightly greased 17 X 11 baking dish.
- Bake in preheated 350 degree oven for 45 minutes or until tender.

Orange Ginger Roasted Apples

Serves 4

Preparation time: 15 minutes
Cooking time: 45–60 minutes

Add a scoop of vanilla bean ice cream and you have dessert.

4 medium Macintosh apples
½ cup honey
¼ cup fresh orange juice
1 teaspoon lemon juice
1 teaspoon grated orange rind
1 teaspoon grated fresh gingerroot
Yogurt or granola for topping

TO MAKE ROASTED APPLES:

- Preheat oven to 400 degrees.
- Core apples, leaving a ½-inch core on the bottom of each apple.
- Place apples in a lightly greased 8 X 8 baking dish.
- Mix honey, orange juice, lemon juice, grated orange rind, and grated fresh gingerroot.
- Drizzle honey mixture over apples, filling centers.
- Bake covered at 400 degrees for 15 minutes.
- Uncover; bake an additional 30–45 minutes.
- Baste every 15 minutes with drippings.
- Remove from baking dish, top with yogurt or granola, and serve immediately.

Not Your Mother's Mac –N– Cheese

Serves 8
Preparation time: 25 minutes
Cooking time: 40 minutes

Definitely an upscale macaroni and cheese dish;
chicken or ham may be added
to make a filling entrée.

16 ounces elbow pasta, cooked and drained
2 ounces Asiago cheese, shredded
2 ounces Gruyére cheese, shredded
2 ounces white Cheddar cheese, shredded
2 ounces Fontina cheese, shredded
2 ounces Gouda cheese, shredded
2 ounces Parmesan cheese, grated
2 ounces blue cheese, crumbled
2 cups milk
1 bay leaf
1 onion quartered
$\frac{1}{2}$ teaspoon nutmeg
4 tablespoons butter
$\frac{1}{4}$ cup flour
1 cup fresh bread crumbs

TO MAKE MACARONI:

◆ Preheat oven to 350 degrees.
◆ Mix the cheeses thoroughly; set aside.
◆ Mix milk, bay leaf, onion, and nutmeg; bring to a simmer; simmer two to three minutes.
◆ Melt butter in a separate saucepan; add flour and cook over low heat for two to three minutes.
◆ Remove flour mixture from heat.
◆ Pour milk mixture very slowly through a strainer into flour mixture.
◆ Mix milk mixture completely into the flour mixture.
◆ After the milk is added, cook over low heat for two to three minutes.
◆ Grease a 3-quart baking dish.
◆ Place one-third of cooked elbow pasta on bottom of baking dish.
◆ Sprinkle with 1 cup of the cheese mixture.
◆ Add layer of elbow pasta, followed by a layer of cheese, followed by elbow pasta, ending with cheese.
◆ Pour milk and flour mixture over pasta.
◆ Let it soak down into the pasta.
◆ Insert a wooden spoon into the pasta to create a small hole so the sauce will sink in. This should be done in several different places. Do not mix or fold the mixture. You want to leave it in layers.
◆ Sprinkle top of pasta with fresh bread crumbs.
◆ Spray top of bread crumbs with butter-flavored cooking spray.
◆ Bake in preheated 350 degree oven for 40 minutes or until hot and bubbly.

Holiday Charm Menu
(Holiday celebrations year-round)

◆

Champagne Fondue or Mariner Mussels in Cider and Cream
Pair with Ingleside Plantation Vineyards Brut Sparkling Wine
or Breaux Vineyards Seyval Blanc

◆

Barboursville Vineyards' White Wine Spinach
Chicken in Phyllo with Shrimp, Feta, and Olives
No Bother Rolls
Oasis Winery's Mushroom Risotto
Pair with Horton Cellars Winery Spotswood Chardonnay
or Oasis Winery Riesling

◆

Berry Tart with Mascarpone Cream
Pair with Oakencroft Vineyard & Winery NV Sweet Virginia
or Oasis Winery Riesling

Desserts

Section photograph dedicated to:
JLNVB Sustainers

Oh, how grand are these holidays
No matter how many there are.
May we continue to gather together
and never be too far.
This day has special charm,
One you'll want to keep,
Old friends, new friends around
sharing in this peace.

—*Toast written by Barrett Bussard, JLNVB member*

Chocolate Butterfinger® Crème Brulee

Advance preparation required.

Serves **8**

Preparation time: 50 minutes
Cooking time: 60 minutes

Say farewell to your traditional crème brulee with this unforgettable, rich combination of sweets.

2⅓ cups heavy cream
¼ teaspoon salt
1⅓ cups milk
⅔ cup sugar
8 ounces semisweet chocolate, melted
10 egg yolks, beaten lightly
1 teaspoon vanilla extract
2 teaspoons bourbon
4.2 ounces Butterfinger® candy bars
Sugar

TO MAKE CRÈME BRULEE:

◆ Place heavy cream, salt, milk, and sugar in a saucepan; heat to just below boiling point.

◆ Pour melted chocolate into cream mixture; stir until smooth.

◆ Stir ¼ cup hot cream and chocolate mixture into beaten eggs, stirring constantly with a spoon. This tempers the eggs and keeps them from becoming scrambled eggs.

◆ Do not whisk; this will cause unwanted air bubbles.

◆ Stir tempered egg mixture into hot cream mixture; blend well.

◆ Strain egg milk mixture into a clean bowl; chill thoroughly by placing the bowl containing the egg mixture in the refrigerator or into a large bowl holding ice water.

◆ Add vanilla extract and bourbon when cooled; store in refrigerator until ready to bake.

◆ Chop Butterfingers® candy bars and distribute into eight 4-ounce individual baking dishes when ready to bake.

◆ Preheat oven to 375 degrees.

◆ Pour custard over candy; fill completely.

◆ Place individual baking dishes in deep pan.

◆ Pour warm water into pan, filling only half the outside depth of baking dishes to make a water bath for cooking.

◆ Cover entire pan with foil.

◆ Bake in preheated 375 degree oven for approximately 60 minutes or until custard is set.

◆ Cool custard to room temperature; refrigerate until thoroughly chilled.

◆ Sprinkle sugar evenly on top of custard and caramelize with propane torch when ready to serve.

Berry Tart with Mascarpone Cream

Advance preparation required.

Serves 6–8

Preparation time: 25 minutes
Cooking time: 30 minutes

Beautiful presentation with an undoubtedly delicious taste.

Refrigerated pie dough
1 cup mascarpone cheese
⅓ cup heavy cream, well chilled
¼ cup sugar
1½ cups small strawberries
1 cup raspberries
1 cup blueberries
1 cup blackberries
2 tablespoons sweet orange marmalade
2 tablespoons dark berry liqueur such as creme de cassis
   or Chambord

TO MAKE TART:

◆ Preheat oven to 375 degrees.

◆ Fit dough into 9-inch tart pan with removable rim.

◆ Trim dough from edges of pan.

◆ Prick entire bottom of dough with a fork.

◆ Line dough with aluminum foil; sprinkle pie weights or raw rice over aluminum foil.

◆ Bake dough in middle of preheated 375 degree oven for 20 minutes.

◆ Carefully remove weights or rice from dough.

◆ Bake an additional 10 minutes or until golden brown.

◆ Cool pastry shell completely.

◆ Cooked pastry shell may be made a day ahead, kept in pan, loosely covered at room temperature.

◆ Beat mascarpone cheese, heavy cream, and sugar in a bowl with whisk or electric mixer until stiff peaks form.

◆ Spoon mascarpone mixture into baked, cooled pastry shell; spread evenly over pastry shell.

◆ Cut strawberries into quarters.

◆ Mix strawberries, raspberries, blueberries, and blackberries in a large bowl.

◆ Simmer orange marmalade and liqueur in a small saucepan.

◆ Stir and cook until volume is reduced to approximately 3 tablespoons.

◆ Pour over berries.

◆ Gently stir berries with a rubber spatula to coat evenly with marmalade mixture.

◆ Mound berries over mascarpone mixture.

◆ Bring tart to room temperature and remove sides of pan before serving.

◆ Tart may be assembled two hours ahead and chilled.

Tantalizing Toffee Cheesecake

Advance preparation required.

Serves 12
Preparation time: 45 minutes
Cooking time: 50 minutes

The outstanding taste will delight everyone.

TOFFEE
 1 cup sugar
 1 cup butter
 ¾ cup chopped pecans, toasted

CRUST
 1 cup chocolate cookie crumbs
 3 tablespoons sugar
 4 tablespoons butter, melted

FILLING
 24 ounces cream cheese, softened
 1 cup sugar
 3 eggs
 1 tablespoon vanilla extract
 1 cup sour cream

TO MAKE TOFFEE:
◆ Melt sugar and butter in a saucepan over medium heat.
◆ Bring butter and sugar to a boil, stirring often, until it reaches a hard crack stage, 300–310 degrees (you must use a candy thermometer).
◆ Watch carefully and do not burn.
◆ Stir pecans into butter mixture; stir well.
◆ Pour mixture quickly onto lightly greased 15 X 10 X 1 baking dish.
◆ Let cool, score top, cool completely, and crack into pieces.

TO MAKE CRUST:
◆ Make the crust for the cheesecake while toffee is setting.
◆ Mix chocolate cookie crumbs and sugar.
◆ Stir melted butter into cookie crumb mixture; mix thoroughly.
◆ Preheat oven to 375 degrees.
◆ Spray 9-inch springform pan with nonstick cooking spray.
◆ Pat cookie crumb mixture into springform pan; bake in preheated 375 degree oven for seven minutes.
◆ Let crust cool before adding cheesecake mixture.

TO MAKE FILLING:
◆ Mix cream cheese and sugar with electric mixer at low speed; mix eggs in one at a time.
◆ Mix in vanilla extract and sour cream.
◆ Do not overbeat.
◆ Preheat oven to 325 degrees.
◆ Place half of cooled toffee in a food processor and process for a rough chop.
◆ Mix 2 cups roughly chopped toffee into cheesecake mixture.
◆ Pour into cooled crust.

Continued on next page...

continued from page 138:

- Bake in preheated 325 degree oven for 40 minutes.
- Process remaining toffee to a fine chop while cheesecake is baking.
- When top of cheesecake is set, approximately 40 minutes of cooking time, sprinkle finely chopped toffee on top of cheesecake; continue cooking for an additional 10 minutes.
- Remove from oven.
- Cool at room temperature for 60 minutes.
- Place in refrigerator for at least two hours before serving.

Pineapple Cheesecake

Advance preparation required.

Serves 8
Preparation time: 30 minutes
Cooking time: 30 minutes

Tantalize your palate with this wonderful blend of flavors.

CRUST
16 graham crackers, crushed
4 tablespoons butter, melted

FILLING
12 ounces cream cheese, softened
1 egg
16 ounces crushed pineapple (minus ½ cup), drained well
1 teaspoon lemon juice
¾ cup sugar
½ cup milk
2 teaspoons vanilla extract

TOPPING
16 ounces sour cream
3 tablespoons sugar
2 teaspoons vanilla extract

TO MAKE CRUST:
- Mix graham crackers and butter; press onto bottom of 8-inch springform pan.
- Preheat oven to 325 degrees.

TO MAKE FILLING:
- Mix cream cheese, egg, pineapple, lemon juice, sugar, milk, and vanilla extract in a bowl; mix thoroughly until smooth.
- Spread mixture evenly over graham cracker crust.
- Bake in preheated 325 degree oven for 20 minutes.
- Remove from oven; cool for 30 minutes.

TO MAKE TOPPING:
- Mix sour cream, sugar, and vanilla extract; mix thoroughly.
- Spread evenly over cool cake.
- Bake an additional 10 minutes in 325 degree oven.
- Remove cheesecake from oven; allow to cool to room temperature.
- Place cheesecake in refrigerator; chill for at least two hours before serving.

Chocolate Kahlua® Cheesecake

Advance preparation required.

Serves 12
Preparation time: 30 minutes
Cooking time: 50 minutes

For best results, make this recipe a day ahead. To prevent condensation from forming on the cake, place a piece of cardboard over top of cake while in refrigerator.

CRUST
  4 tablespoons butter, melted
  1 cup fine graham cracker crumbs
  ⅛ cup sugar
FILLING
  32 ounces cream cheese, softened
  1½ cups sugar
  1 teaspoon vanilla extract
  1 teaspoon almond extract
  Pinch of salt
  4 eggs
  8 ounces semisweet chocolate
  1 tablespoon Kahlua®
TOPPING
  ¾ cup sour cream
  ¼ cup sugar
  ½ teaspoon almond extract
  1 teaspoon Kahlua®

TO MAKE CRUST:
◆ Mix butter, graham cracker crumbs, and sugar until completely blended.
◆ Press into bottom of 9-inch springform pan.
◆ Preheat oven 350 degrees.

TO MAKE FILLING:
◆ Mix cream cheese and sugar; beat with electric mixer for two minutes.
◆ Mix in vanilla extract, almond extract, and salt; blend thoroughly.
◆ Mix eggs one at a time into cream cheese mixture using lowest speed of mixer.
◆ Mix until eggs are just mixed into the batter.
◆ Pour two-thirds of batter into graham cracker crust; set aside remaining batter.
◆ Melt chocolate in double boiler; pour Kahlua® into chocolate; mix well.
◆ Pour chocolate mixture into reserved third of batter; blend.
◆ Spoon chocolate batter one spoonful at a time into middle of batter already in pan.
◆ After all the chocolate has been spooned over the batter, use a knife to swirl the chocolate through the batter.
◆ Bake in preheated 350 degree oven for 40 minutes.
◆ Take cheesecake out of oven for 10 minutes.
◆ Make topping while cheesecake cools.

continued on next page...

continued from page 140:

TO MAKE TOPPING:

- Mix sour cream, sugar, almond extract, and Kahlua®.
- Spread topping evenly over top of baked filling.
- Return to oven for an additional 10 minutes.
- Remove from oven; place cheesecake in refrigerator immediately to cool.
- Place a piece of cardboard over top of cake while in refrigerator to prevent condensation from forming on cake.
- Refrigerate several hours to chill thoroughly before serving.

Beach Balls

Advance preparation required.

Yields 10 dozen 1-inch balls
Preparation time: 60 minutes

An irresistible dessert that makes an unforgettable gift.

1 cup finely chopped pecans
½ cup bourbon
8 tablespoons butter, softened
1 tablespoon vanilla extract
1 teaspoon salt
14 ounces sweetened condensed milk
2 pounds plus 2 cups confectioners sugar
1½ pounds dark or milk chocolate, melted

TO MAKE BEACH BALLS:

- Soak pecans in bourbon for three hours or overnight, stirring occasionally.
- Beat butter, vanilla extract, and salt in a large mixer until fluffy.
- Gradually beat sweetened condensed milk into butter mixture.
- Stir pecans and bourbon into butter mixture; mix thoroughly.
- Stir confectioners sugar into butter mixture; beat until well blended.
- Refrigerate mixture for 60 minutes for easier handling.
- Remove from refrigerator; with hands, shape mixture into 1-inch balls; place on a cookie sheet.
- Refrigerate until firm (several hours).
- Melt chocolate in double boiler.
- Remove balls from the refrigerator a few at a time; allow the remainder to continue chilling.
- Dip balls into chocolate using candy dipper or two toothpicks or wear thin food-safe plastic gloves.
- Place coated balls back on the cookie sheet lined with wax paper; refrigerate.
- Store in refrigerator or freezer.

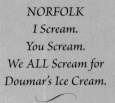

Almond Chocolate Torte

Serves **8**

Preparation time: 40 minutes
Cooking time: 45 minutes

The smooth rich taste makes this dessert worth the effort.

TORTE
Boiling water
6 ounces unblanched almonds
2 ounces shelled walnuts
1 cup sugar, plus one heaping teaspoon sugar
16 tablespoons butter, softened
6 eggs, separated
1 teaspoon orange extract
½ teaspoon vanilla extract
9 ounces bittersweet chocolate
2 whole eggs

TOPPING
2 cups heavy cream
1 tablespoon sugar
1 teaspoon confectioners sugar

GARNISH
Grated peel of large orange
½ cup sugar

TO MAKE TORTE:

◆ Preheat oven to 375 degrees.

◆ Butter and flour bottom and sides of 10-inch cake pan; place a piece of parchment paper on the bottom of prepared cake pan.

◆ Pour boiling water over almonds.

◆ Let almonds stand in water for NO more than 60 seconds.

◆ Drain hot water from almonds.

◆ Pour cold water over almonds.

◆ Drain water again from almonds; blot almonds dry with a paper towel.

◆ Spread dry almonds on a cookie sheet and bake in preheated 375 degree oven for 20 minutes.

◆ Remove almonds from oven.

◆ Place almonds and walnuts in a food processor with 1 cup sugar; process until finely ground.

◆ Cream butter with electric mixer; mix egg yolks in one at a time.

◆ Stir in ground nuts 1 teaspoon at a time followed by orange and vanilla extracts.

◆ Melt bittersweet chocolate in double boiler; cool.

◆ Stir melted chocolate into creamed butter mixture.

◆ Mix whole eggs into chocolate mixture; mix for one minute.

◆ Whisk 6 egg whites and remaining 1 teaspoon sugar until stiff peaks form.

◆ Gently fold egg whites into batter with a rubber spatula.

◆ Turn oven heat down to 350 degrees.

Continued on next page...

continued from page 142:

TO MAKE TORTE:

◆ Pour batter into prepared pan; bake in preheated 350 degree oven for 45 minutes.

◆ Top of torte should be lightly crusted and the sides detached from the pan, but soft to the touch.

◆ Let torte rest on a rack for 15 minutes.

◆ Unmold torte onto serving platter.

◆ Cover with a metal bowl; let cool completely before serving.

TO MAKE TOPPING:

◆ Prepare topping when ready to serve torte.

◆ Whip heavy cream, sugar, and confectioners sugar in a chilled bowl until soft peaks form.

◆ Slice the torte into wedges.

TO MAKE GARNISH:

◆ Mix orange peel and sugar.

◆ Serve torte topped with whipped cream; sprinkled whipped cream with orange peel and sugar mixture.

Chocolate Truffles

Advance preparation required.

Yields approximately 6 dozen 1-inch balls
Preparation time: 40 minutes

For an attractive presentation, arrange on a plate with strawberries after drizzling with white chocolate.

1 pound 2 ounces Oreo™ cookies, finely crushed
8 ounces cream cheese, softened
2 tablespoons Grand Marnier® liqueur, optional
10 ounces German chocolate
2 tablespoons paramount crystals (found in candy supply store)
4 ounces white chocolate, melted

TO MAKE TRUFFLES:

◆ Mix Oreo™ cookies and cream cheese with an electric mixer on slow speed until completely mixed.

◆ Stir Grand Marnier® liqueur into cookie crumb mixture; mix again.

◆ Roll mixture into small balls.

◆ Place balls on a cookie sheet lined with waxed paper; freeze for several hours.

◆ Place German chocolate in a double boiler over low heat; melt.

◆ Stir paramount crystals into German chocolate, as needed, to thin German chocolate for dipping.

◆ Remove balls from freezer; dip in melted chocolate, covering completely.

◆ Place chocolate-covered balls back on a cookie sheet lined with waxed paper; return to freezer.

◆ Drizzle firm chocolate balls with melted white chocolate for garnish.

◆ Store in freezer in a freezer-safe container until ready to serve. The chocolate truffles thaw quickly.

No Bake Chocolate Delicacy

Advance preparation required.

Serves 30
Preparation time: 45 minutes

A chocolate lover's dream recipe.

LAYER

2 cups semisweet morsels

1 cup sour cream

Dash salt

8 tablespoons margarine

2 cups confectioners sugar

4 cups vanilla wafer crumbs, approximately 120 cookies

2 cups finely chopped walnuts

FILLING

10 tablespoons margarine, softened

2½ tablespoons milk

2½ cups confectioners sugar

½ teaspoon peppermint extract

FROSTING

1 cup semisweet morsels

½ cup sweetened condensed milk

1½ teaspoons vanilla extract

Chopped nuts for garnish

TO MAKE LAYER:

◆ Butter the sides of two 9-inch cake pans; line bottoms of cake pans with wax or parchment paper.

◆ Melt semisweet morsels in a double boiler; remove from heat.

◆ Stir sour cream and salt into melted chocolate; set aside.

◆ Melt margarine in a medium-size saucepan; stir in confectioners sugar, vanilla wafer crumbs, and walnuts; mix thoroughly.

◆ Stir melted chocolate morsel mixture into confectioners sugar mixture and mix thoroughly.

◆ Spread batter evenly into two prepared cake pans; chill several hours.

◆ Make filling next.

TO MAKE FILLING:

◆ Mix margarine, milk, confectioners sugar, and peppermint extract in a medium-size bowl.

◆ Beat on high with an electric mixer until well mixed.

◆ Remove one layer from cake pan onto a serving plate; spread filling evenly over layer.

◆ Remove second layer from cake pan; place second layer over filled base layer.

◆ Chill until filling is firm.

◆ Make frosting.

TO MAKE FROSTING:

◆ Melt semisweet morsels in a small saucepan over low heat; add condensed milk, stirring constantly.

Continued on next page...

continued from page 144:

TO MAKE FROSTING:

◆ Stir in vanilla extract.

◆ Spread frosting over top layer.

◆ Sprinkle top with finely chopped nuts for garnish.

◆ Store in refrigerator.

Orange Brickle Pie

Advance preparation required.

Serves 10

Preparation time: 30 minutes
Cooking time: 8–10 minutes for crust,
12–15 minutes for filling

Refreshingly flavorful.

CRUST

1¼ cups graham cracker crumbs

¼ cup sugar

⅓ cup butter, softened

FILLING

¾ cup sugar

6 tablespoons butter

¼ cup frozen orange juice concentrate, thawed

2 tablespoons water

Dash salt

2 eggs, beaten

1 quart vanilla ice cream

2 tablespoons orange liqueur

2 oranges, sliced

TO MAKE CRUST:

◆ Preheat oven to 350 degrees.

◆ Combine graham cracker crumbs, sugar, and butter; press firmly into bottom and sides of a 9-inch pan.

◆ Bake in 350 degree oven for 8–10 minutes.

TO MAKE FILLING:

◆ Mix sugar, butter, orange juice concentrate, water, salt, and eggs in a saucepan.

◆ Cook over low heat, stirring occasionally until mixture bubbles.

◆ Simmer for an additional two minutes, stirring constantly.

◆ Place clear plastic wrap directly onto surface of cooked orange mixture; chill in refrigerator for several hours.

◆ Soften half of ice cream in a bowl; work ice cream with a wooden spoon until just pliable.

◆ Spread ice cream into baked graham cracker crust using a metal spatula.

◆ Quickly top with orange mixture; freeze until firm.

◆ Soften remaining ice cream; stir in orange liqueur.

◆ Spread over frozen mixture; freeze several hours or overnight.

◆ Ice cream will not freeze firm.

◆ Serve immediately from freezer.

◆ Top with orange slices.

What's of legal age, invites 190,000 visitors, and is red all over? The Pungo Strawberry Festival, of course. This two-day annual festival began in 1983 and has been a big hit ever since. It's located just a few miles south of Virginia Beach's oceanfront in the lush farmland section of the city called Pungo.

For decades, locals, tourists, and Tidewater neighbors have been spending their Memorial Day weekend knee deep in strawberries. You can pick your own or sample more than 50 tempting strawberry dishes.

In addition to eating strawberries to your heart's content, there are plenty of things to see and do: a pie eating contest (strawberry, of course), strawberry bake off, racing car exhibits, carnival games and rides, musical entertainment on four stages, a parade, livestock sale and show, impressive military display, pig races, a youth art show, and a unique arts and crafts exhibit. Kick off your summer with a day at the Pungo Strawberry Festival. You'll be glad you did.

Mermaid's Margarita Pie

Advance preparation required.

Serves **6**
Preparation time: 10 minutes
Cooking time: 15 minutes

For added presentation, garnish with lime wedges.

4 egg yolks
14 ounces sweetened condensed milk
⅓ cup fresh lime juice
2 tablespoons tequila
1 tablespoon triple sec
4 tablespoons minced lime zest
9-inch graham cracker pie crust
Whipped cream topping

TO MAKE PIE:

◆ Preheat oven to 350 degrees.
◆ Whisk egg yolks and sweetened condensed milk; stir in lime juice.
◆ Whisk mixture for one minute.
◆ Whisk tequila, triple sec, and lime zest into condensed milk mixture; pour mixture into graham cracker pie crust.
◆ Bake in preheated 350 degree oven until filling is lightly set, approximately 15 minutes.
◆ Cool to room temperature.
◆ Refrigerate at least two hours or until ready to serve.
◆ Top with whipped cream.

Summer Sorbet

Serves **6**
Preparation time: 30 minutes
Cooking time: 10–12 minutes

A simple, refreshingly sweet summer dessert.

⅓ cup sugar
1¼ cups hot water
16 ounces fresh strawberries, sliced
½ cup fresh lemon juice

TO MAKE SORBET:

◆ Mix sugar and hot water; cook over medium heat until sugar is dissolved.
◆ Bring mixture to a boil; boil for five minutes.
◆ Place strawberries in a food processor; process for one minute.
◆ Pour pureed strawberries into a strainer placed over a bowl to catch the juice.
◆ Mix strained strawberries into sugar-water mixture.
◆ Stir fresh lemon juice into strawberry mixture.
◆ Bring entire mixture to a boil; reduce heat and simmer for five to seven minutes.
◆ Strain mixture into a freezer-safe container.
◆ Cover tightly and freeze.
◆ Let sit at room temperature for 20 minutes to soften before serving.

Splendid Strawberry Crêpes

Serves **8**

Preparation time: 30 minutes
Cooking time: 90 seconds

Great for a special occasion brunch.
Sprinkle with confectioners sugar or top with
whipped cream and fresh berries.

CRÊPES

1 cup flour
1 tablespoon sugar
¼ teaspoon salt
1 cup milk
⅓ cup water
3 eggs
3 tablespoons butter, melted

STRAWBERRY FILLING

8 ounces strawberry yogurt
1 cup strawberry preserves
1 pound fresh strawberries, hulled and sliced
Whipping cream

TO MAKE CRÊPES:

◆ Mix flour, sugar, and salt in a food processor until well blended.
◆ Add milk, water, eggs, and butter through the feed tube while food processor is running.
◆ Make sure mixture is well blended.
◆ Use a 7-inch nonstick crêpe pan or a 7-inch nonstick sauté pan with flared sides.
◆ Spray pan with nonstick cooking spray or butter to grease the bottom.
◆ Heat pan on medium to medium-high heat.
◆ When pan starts to smoke slightly, it is hot enough.
◆ Pour ⅓ cup batter into the center of pan and immediately tilt pan from side to side and back to front to spread batter evenly around bottom of pan.
◆ When edges turn brown, approximately one minute, run a spatula under the edge to loosen crêpe.
◆ Flip crêpe over by gently lifting one corner with a spatula.
◆ Lift the opposite corner with your fingers and gently lift and turn the crêpe.
◆ Cook on opposite side for approximately 30 seconds.
◆ Slide crêpe out of pan and onto a sheet of waxed paper.
◆ Place waxed paper between crêpes to keep them from sticking.

TO MAKE FILLING:

◆ Place strawberry yogurt, strawberry preserves, and fresh strawberries in food processor; blend until well mixed, but not completely smooth.
◆ Spoon a large tablespoon of filling into each crêpe.
◆ Fold one edge over about a third of the way, then fold the other over and tuck the end of it under the crêpe.
◆ Garnish with whipped cream.

Pretty & Pink Marble Pound Cake

Serves 12

Preparation time: 30 minutes
Cooking time: 90 minutes

Enhance the attractive look of this cake by serving with fresh sliced strawberries and whipped cream.

CAKE
- 20 tablespoons butter, softened
- 3 cups sugar
- 5 eggs
- 2 teaspoons vanilla extract
- ¼ teaspoon almond extract
- 3 cups flour
- ½ teaspoon baking powder
- 1 cup milk
- Red food coloring
- 2 teaspoons strawberry extract

GLAZE
- ½ cup water
- 1 cup sugar
- 3 teaspoons strawberry extract

TO MAKE CAKE:
- ◆ Preheat oven to 300 degrees.
- ◆ Grease and flour fluted tube pan.
- ◆ Cream butter and sugar with electric mixer; add eggs at low speed one at a time, beating well after each addition.
- ◆ Stir vanilla extract and almond extract into creamed butter mixture; mix well.
- ◆ Sift flour and baking powder together.
- ◆ Stir 1 cup flour into creamed butter mixture; mix well.
- ◆ Stir ¼ cup milk into creamed butter mixture; mix well.
- ◆ Stir remaining flour into creamed butter mixture 1 cup at a time, mixing well; add ¼ cup milk after each cup of flour is blended.
- ◆ Place one-third of batter in a separate bowl; add drops of red food coloring to batter, mixing well until batter turns pink.
- ◆ Stir strawberry extract into pink batter.
- ◆ Pour uncolored batter into prepared fluted tube pan; add pink batter to top of uncolored batter; it will sink naturally.
- ◆ Bake in lower third of a preheated 300 degree oven for 90 minutes.

TO MAKE GLAZE:
- ◆ Mix water, sugar, and strawberry extract in a saucepan over low heat.
- ◆ Heat until sugar is dissolved.
- ◆ Let cool.
- ◆ Remove cake from the oven when finished baking; poke lots of small holes in the top of hot cake.
- ◆ Pour cooled glaze over top of hot cake.
- ◆ Let cake sit for 20 minutes.
- ◆ Remove cake from tube pan and let cool completely.

Banana Pound Cake

Serves **10**

Preparation time: 25 minutes
Cooking time: 1 hour 20 minutes

Bananas liven up this classic dessert.

1 cup shortening
8 tablespoons butter, softened
3 cups sugar
5 eggs
3 ripe bananas, mashed
3 tablespoons milk
2 teaspoons vanilla extract
3 cups flour
½ teaspoon salt
1 teaspoon baking powder

TO MAKE CAKE:

◆ Preheat oven to 350 degrees.
◆ Grease and flour tube pan.
◆ Beat shortening and butter until creamy; mix in sugar and eggs gradually.
◆ Mix bananas, milk, and vanilla extract in a bowl.
◆ Mix flour, salt, and baking powder in a separate bowl.
◆ Stir flour and banana mixture alternately into butter mixture; mix until blended.
◆ Pour batter into prepared tube pan.
◆ Bake in preheated 350 degree oven for 1 hour and 20 minutes.
◆ Remove cake from oven; let cake rest in tube pan for 15 minutes.
◆ Remove cake from tube pan; cool completely before serving.

Trifle a la Viognier from King Family Vineyard

Advance preparation required.

Serves **8**
Preparation time: 15 minutes

16 ounces plain pound cake
1 cup Loreley Late Harvest Viognier
16 ounces heavy cream, whipped
1 tablespoon sugar
1 pint fresh fruit (raspberries, peaches, etc.)

TO MAKE TRIFLE:

◆ Cut pound cake into bite-size pieces; place in a bowl.
◆ Drizzle Loreley Late Harvest Viognier over cake.
◆ Refrigerate cake for several hours, stirring gently occasionally.
◆ Whip cream with electric mixer on low speed until soft peaks form; sprinkle sugar over cream; increase speed of mixer and whip until firm peaks are formed.
◆ Place a layer of pound cake in trifle bowl or individual serving dishes, then a layer of sweetened cream, and then a layer of fresh fruit.
◆ Continue layering until bowl or dishes are full.
◆ Chill and serve.

"First from the sea, first to the stars" is the motto of Hampton, Virginia. Established in 1610, this city has deep historic roots as America's first continuously occupied English-speaking settlement. Today, Hampton is home to the NASA Langley Research Center where the country's first astronauts—Mercury Seven—honed their flight skills.

Hampton's downtown waterfront area has been extensively renovated. Attractions include cobblestone streets, shops, restaurants, galleries, a restored antique carousel, and a waterfront park. Located here is the Royal Customs House, where the British once brought tea and other supplies to the colonists.

The proximity of NASA has brought the Virginia Air and Space Center—the official visitor center for both NASA Langley Research Center and the Langley Air Force Base—to downtown Hampton. Here, you can experience the aura of piloting a shuttle, the excitement of launching a rocket, and the magnificent feeling of flight. Come face-to-face with the Apollo 12 Command Module that went to the moon and view several space artifacts. Visitors can also take in a "space-age" film in the giant Riverside IMAX Theater. From the Air and Space Center, the Langley Motor Tour transports visitors to NASA Langley where our nation's space history began. This tour brings you up close to NASA's giant wind tunnel and the massive scaffolding used for simulated space capsule landings.

One thing is for sure—a visit to this Tidewater city is guaranteed to be uplifting.

Southern Comforting Bread Pudding

Advance preparation required.

Serves 12
Preparation time: 30 minutes
Cooking time: 40 minutes

A new twist to a traditional comfort.

BREAD PUDDING

2 large sweet potatoes, 1½–2 pounds total weight
8 tablespoons butter, divided
16 ounces French bread, torn into pieces and dried on a flat surface for two to four hours
4 cups milk
4 eggs
1 cup sugar
1 tablespoon vanilla extract
1 teaspoon cinnamon

SAUCE

16 tablespoons butter
¾ cup light brown sugar
1 cup chopped pecans or walnuts
¼ cup bourbon

TO MAKE BREAD PUDDING:

◆ Preheat oven to 400 degrees.
◆ Prick sweet potatoes with a fork; bake in preheated 400 degree oven for 60 minutes or until soft.
◆ Scoop out meat of sweet potatoes when sweet potatoes are baked and cool enough to handle.
◆ Butter 13 X 9 X 2 baking dish with 1 tablespoon of butter.
◆ Place dried bread in baking dish.
◆ Tuck sweet potatoes between torn pieces of bread.
◆ Mash mixture down with a fork.
◆ Beat together milk, eggs, sugar, vanilla extract, and cinnamon; pour over bread and sweet potatoes.
◆ Let soak at room temperature for three hours.
◆ Preheat oven to 375 degrees.
◆ Cut remaining 7 tablespoons butter into small pieces; sprinkle over bread and sweet potatoes.
◆ Bake in preheated 375 degree oven for 40 minutes.
◆ Let cool for 30 minutes.
◆ Make sauce while bread pudding cools.

TO MAKE SAUCE:

◆ Melt butter in a saucepan; stir in brown sugar; mix until mixture begins to boil.
◆ Stir nuts and bourbon into butter mixture.
◆ Spoon hot sauce over cooled bread pudding.

Zuppa Inglese

Advance preparation required.

Serves 6

Preparation time: 30 minutes

For a fantastic finish, garnish with whipped cream and chocolate shavings.

2 cups half-and-half
3 egg yolks
¾ cup confectioners sugar
5 tablespoons flour
1 teaspoon grated lemon rind
½ cup whipping cream
4 ounces semisweet white chocolate morsels
10¾ ounces frozen pound cake
½ cup Amaretto liqueur
Whipped cream and white chocolate shavings, for garnish

TO MAKE ZUPPA:

◆ Whisk half-and-half, egg yolks, confectioners sugar, and flour in a heavy saucepan until blended.
◆ Cook over medium heat, whisking often, approximately 15 minutes or until thickened.
◆ Stir in lemon rind; set aside.
◆ Mix whipping cream and semisweet white chocolate morsels in a small bowl; microwave on high for one minute.
◆ Stir until smooth.
◆ Cut pound cake into thin slices; drizzle with Amaretto liqueur.
◆ Pour custard into serving glasses (six 10-ounce compotes or wine glasses) and add cake pieces.
◆ Chill two hours.
◆ Garnish with whipped cream and white chocolate shavings and serve.

Tidewater Toffee

Serves 12

Preparation time: 10 minutes
Cooking time: 20 minutes

Macadamia nuts are a nice substitute when making this easy and fun recipe.

2 cups sugar
1 pound butter (do not substitute margarine)
1½ cups chopped pecans, toasted

TO MAKE TOFFEE:

◆ Melt sugar and butter in a saucepan over medium heat.
◆ Bring to a boil, stirring often; bring temperature of mixture to hard crack stage of 300–310 degrees (you must use a candy thermometer).
◆ Watch carefully and do not burn.
◆ Stir chopped and toasted pecans into butter and sugar mixture; mix well.
◆ Pour quickly onto a lightly greased 15 X 10 X 1 baking pan.
◆ Cool to the touch; score top.
◆ Cool completely and crack into pieces.

Pecan Pie with Kahlua® & Chocolate Chips

Advance preparation required.

Serves *8*

Preparation time: 30 minutes
Cooking time: 45 minutes

½ cup sugar
4 tablespoon unsalted butter, softened
1 tablespoon flour
¾ cup dark corn syrup
¼ cup Kahlua®
1 teaspoon vanilla extract
3 eggs, beaten
1 cup chopped pecans
½ cup semisweet morsels
9-inch pie crust
Whipped cream
Pecan halves

TO MAKE PIE:

◆ Preheat oven to 375 degrees.

◆ Beat sugar and butter in medium bowl until smooth; stir in flour.

◆ Gradually stir corn syrup, Kahlua®, and vanilla extract into butter mixture.

◆ Mix eggs and chopped pecans into mixture.

◆ Sprinkle semisweet morsels over bottom of pie crust.

◆ Pour filling over semisweet morsels.

◆ Bake pie in preheated 375 degree oven for approximately 45 minutes or until filling is puffed around edges and just set in center; cover edge of crust with aluminum if browning too quickly.

◆ Transfer pie to rack to cool; do not cover; allow to sit out overnight uncovered to set properly.

◆ Cover and store in refrigerator after pie is set.

◆ Top with whipped cream and pecan halves to serve.

Pumpkin Pecan Pie

Serves 12
Preparation time: 20 minutes
Cooking time: 45 minutes

Easy to prepare and tastes wonderful.

PIE

- ½ teaspoon salt
- ¾ cup sugar
- 1 teaspoon cinnamon
- ½ teaspoon ground ginger
- ¼ teaspoon ground cloves
- 2 eggs
- 15 ounces canned pumpkin
- 2 cups evaporated milk
- 9-inch pie crust

PECAN TOPPING

- 1 egg
- 2 tablespoons dark corn syrup
- 2 tablespoons firmly packed brown sugar
- 1 tablespoon butter, melted
- 1 teaspoon maple extract (brandy or rum extract can be substituted)
- 1 cup chopped pecans

TO MAKE PIE:

- ◆ Preheat oven to 425 degrees.
- ◆ Mix salt, sugar, cinnamon, ginger, and cloves; stir in eggs and pumpkin.
- ◆ Add evaporated milk gradually; mix well; pour into pie crust.
- ◆ Bake in preheated 425 degree oven for 20 minutes.
- ◆ Remove pie from oven; lower oven temperature to 350 degrees.

TO MAKE PECAN TOPPING:

- ◆ Mix egg, corn syrup, brown sugar, butter, maple extract, and pecans; spoon evenly over baked pie.
- ◆ Pie may appear to sink.
- ◆ Return pie to oven.
- ◆ Bake in a 350 degree oven for an additional 25 minutes.

Sustainer's Holiday Cake

Serves 8–12

Preparation time: 20 minutes
Cooking time: 60 minutes

The cranberries and chocolate create a satisfying contrast in flavor.

CAKE
- 2¼ cups flour
- 1 cup sugar
- 1 teaspoon baking powder
- 1 teaspoon baking soda
- ⅛ teaspoon salt
- 2 eggs
- ¾ cup oil
- 1 cup buttermilk
- 1 cup whole fresh cranberries, or dried if not in season (see prep tip)
- 1 cup chocolate chips
- 1 cup pecans, chopped
- 1 cup dates, chopped

GLAZE
- 8 ounces confectioners sugar
- 2 tablespoons orange juice
- 1 teaspoon orange peel

TO MAKE CAKE:
- ◆ Preheat oven to 350 degrees.
- ◆ Grease and flour fluted tube pan.
- ◆ Mix flour, sugar, baking powder, baking soda, and salt.
- ◆ Mix eggs, oil, and buttermilk in a separate bowl with an electric mixer on low speed.
- ◆ Slowly add flour mixture to egg mixture; mix well, approximately two minutes.
- ◆ Stir cranberries, chocolate chips, pecans, and dates into batter.
- ◆ Pour batter into prepared greased and floured fluted tube pan.
- ◆ Bake in preheated 350 degree oven for 60 minutes or until done.
- ◆ Cool for 15 minutes in pan.
- ◆ Remove cake from fluted tube pan.

TO MAKE GLAZE:
- ◆ Mix confectioners sugar, orange juice, and orange peel until smooth; pour over cake.

- ◆ *Prep Tip:* If you are using dried cranberries, soak in 2 tablespoons of brandy for 30 minutes; drain brandy and dust with small amount of flour, shaking off excess flour before adding to batter.

Coconut Macaroons

Yields approximately 2 dozen cookies
Preparation time: 15 minutes
Cooking time: 20 minutes

**Using parchment paper will make removal of
the cooked macaroons easier.**

⅓ cup flour
½ teaspoon salt
4 cups grated coconut
¾ cup sweetened condensed milk
1 teaspoon vanilla extract
8 ounces dark chocolate

TO MAKE MACAROONS:

◆ Preheat oven to 350 degrees.
◆ Grease two baking sheets.
◆ Sift flour and salt into a bowl; stir coconut into flour.
◆ Pour sweetened condensed milk into flour mixture followed by vanilla extract; stir from the center until a thick mixture is formed.
◆ Drop tablespoonfuls of the mixture 1 inch apart on the baking sheets.
◆ Bake in preheated 350 degree oven for approximately 20 minutes or until golden brown.
◆ Cool macaroons on a wire rack.
◆ Melt dark chocolate in a double boiler over simmering water.
◆ Spread melted dark chocolate over bottoms of macaroons; let chocolate harden.
◆ Store in refrigerator or freezer.

.

from First Colony Winery:
First Colony Blueberries

Advance preparation required.

Serves 4
Preparation time: 10 minutes
Cooking time: 30–45 minutes

Delicious and healthy, too!

8 ounces fresh blueberries
1 bottle (375ml) First Colony Winery Late Harvest Vidal Blanc

TO MAKE BLUEBERRIES:

◆ Mix blueberries and wine in a medium saucepan.
◆ Bring to a boil; reduce to a simmer.
◆ Reduce sauce by two-thirds of the original amount of liquid; this will take 30–45 minutes depending on your simmer.
◆ Chill several hours.
◆ Serve over coconut or vanilla sorbet with a glass of First Colony Late Harvest Vidal Blanc.

Our Wine Pairings

The wines, beers, and ciders suggested in this cookbook are just that—suggestions. The selected beverages were paired to the recipes by a panel of beverage experts using but a representation of the offerings produced throughout Virginia.

These pairings were made using vintages and brews available at the time of this cookbook's printing. As vintages change, so do flavors and tastes. Therefore, we have also included tasting notes in the hopes that future readers will be able to use these suggestions as a starting point in their discovery of Virginia wines, beers, and ciders.

Our panel agreed that in matching these beverages and recipes they not only experienced delicious Virginia food and wines that brought out the best in each other, but also passionate people who did the same. Above all else, camaraderie is the table's greatest harvest.

Wine Panel Biographies

SHARON BRADSHAW

Ms. Bradshaw is certified by the Society of Wine Educators and is a consultant to the Virginia Wine of the Month Club, for which she also writes a monthly newsletter. Ms. Bradshaw is a co-founder of Hartwood Winery, a charter member of the Fredericksburg Wine Society, and a past president and newsletter editor for the Virginia Vineyards Association. She is a co-founder of the Fredericksburg Area Wine Festival and currently serves as vice-president to the Vinifera Wine Growers Association.

HANK FOILES III

Mr. Foiles has been educating consumers on wine since 1972. He worked for Vintage Imports under the guidance of Norman Garret as well as local beverages companies including Chesapeake Bay Wine Co., Tri-Cities Beverage, and Associated Distributors. He currently works for Country Vintner located in Oilville, Virginia. Hank has been the guest speaker and consultant for more than 100 wine dinners in the local area. He has traveled throughout Europe to further his education and interest in fine wines.

MARISA ALMA MARSEY

Ms. Marsey is a recruiter for Johnson & Wales Culinary Arts University and a Virginia Press award-winning food writer. Her work appears in numerous publications and she is a regular contributor to Hampton Road's *Port Folio Weekly*. Ms. Marsey is also involved with the Chesapeake Bay Wine Classic and the Town Point Virginia Wine Competition.

TOMAS RODRIGUEZ

Mr. Rodriguez is managing director of La Provencale Cellars, a wine importing and marketing organization. He is a charter member of the board of directors of the Fredericksburg Area Wine festival and is the founder and president of the Washington Area International Wine Festival. Mr. Rodriguez also serves on the board of directors of the Vinifera Wine Growers Association and of the Fredericksburg Area Wine Festival.

ANDREÃ SIMEK

Ms. Simek is a private wine consultant and area sales representative for The Robins Cellars Wine Distributor of Richmond, Virginia. She previously owned a wine shop in Virginia Beach, and has taught at Johnson & Wales Culinary Arts University in Norfolk. Ms. Simek has appeared on the Local News Channel (LNC) and the WTKR Channel 3 Morning Show as a consultant on food and wine pairings.

MARI SPRAGINS

Ms. Spragins is co-owner and wine consultant of Ye Olde Dominion Wine Shoppe in Historic Occoquan, Virginia. Ye Olde Dominion Wine Shoppe is the first, exclusively "all Virginia" retail wine establishment in Virginia and is the winner of the 2002 Wine Retailer of the Year Award. Ms. Spragins is a member of the Society of Wine Educators, the Prince William Chamber of Commerce, and Empire's Who's Who.

KELLY THOMPSON

Ms. Thompson has been an authority on the hospitality business for more than 25 years. She has organized, prepared, and paired food for more than 75 wine tastings. Ms. Thompson has worked for Broudy-Kantor Wine and Beverage Distributor for three years and, previously was co-owner of Bay Gourmet, Specialty Wine and Gourmet Deli.

WINE PAIRING TIPS

Sharon believes that there are enough good wines to pair with any given dish or meal that everyone's palate can be pleased. She says sampling wine at festivals, store tastings, wine clubs, or at the winery is an excellent way to discover what you enjoy and fill your wine cellar with favorites.

Hank has never met a wine he didn't like.

Marisa's personal philosophy of wine pairing is simple: Approach every meal with an open mind and an open mouth and you always will come away with a blissfully full heart. While there may be ideal matches, when it comes to marrying food and wine, Marisa believes in polygamy.

Tom believes that personal preference rules in food and wine pairing. If you like them together, then they go together. He says the challenge is to become familiar with as many foods and wines as possible to allow you to make great combinations.

Andréa feels that you truly can't enjoy good food without enjoying good wine. In life she believes everything has a perfect match, and this is true of food and wine. The harmonious complement of a well-paired food and wine is a glorious assault on the senses.

Although Mari personally believes that some foods may indicate a specific wine pairing, she believes that daring experimentation often offers unexpected—and wonderful—surprises. She believes that the ultimate pleasure lies on the palate of the individual.

Kelly offers this piece of advice: If you find yourself attending a dinner and don't know what is being served, bring a bottle of your favorite Sauvignon Blanc. It is a versatile wine that pairs well with anything. She says the bottom line is that what you enjoy will always be the best choice.

Wine Tasting Notes

To assist in finding a replacement, if a Virginia product is unavailable.

ALPENGLOW CIDERS

◆ **Classic Blush** – This full-bodied cider has a delicate blush color and is made from Virginia grown rougeon and muscadine grapes.

◆ **Sparkling Cider** – This blend of several varieties of fresh apples provides a crisp, clear, nonalcoholic taste sensation.

BARBOURSVILLE VINEYARDS

◆ **Brut** – This is a classic blend of carefully selected Chardonnay and Pinot Noir grapes. Refreshing vibrant fruit flavors lead to ripe pear that lingers on the finish. The moderate acidity integrates well with fine bubbles and a soft structure.

◆ **Sangiovese Reserve** – Gentle and elegant, this wine has plenty of cherry and plum aromas that are well-integrated with a lingering finish and a round structure.

◆ **Chardonnay** – Cold fermentation in stainless steel yields this fresh wine with crisp acidity and clean varietal flavors of apple, pear, and lemon.

BREAUX VINEYARDS

◆ **Cabernet Sauvignon** – Dark-hued and rich, this earthy red is full of currant and raspberry flavors. A velvety finish leaves hints of spice. This wine has an aging potential of 5 to 10 years.

◆ **Lafayette Cabernet Franc** – A mix of 75 percent Cabernet Franc, 15 percent Cabernet Sauvignon, and 10 percent Merlot, this wine is a spicy medium-bodied red with plum and dark cherry flavors. It has a spicy and flavorful finish.

◆ **Barrel-Fermented Chardonnay** – A complex wine with toasty, roasted flavors that come from the French oak barrels. The wine is soft, creamy, and somewhat buttery as a result of partial malolactic fermentation.

◆ **Sauvignon Blanc** – This wine has varietal herbal qualities with hints of citrus, grapefruit, and pineapple.

◆ **Seyval Blanc** – This wine is crisp and dry with hints of green apple and grapefruit, as well as firm acidity.

CARDINAL POINT VINEYARD & WINERY

◆ **Cabernet Sauvignon** – This is a lighter Cabernet Sauvignon with considerable depth. It is supple with hints of vanilla and strawberry.

◆ **A6** – This fruity blend of 54 percent Chardonnay and 46 percent Viognier is 100 percent barrel fermented. There is a welcome combination of the oak creaminess of Chardonnay and "fruit-first" palate of Viognier.

CHATEAU MORRISETTE

◆ **Frosty Dog** – This wine is tropical, sweet, and fruity.

◆ **Our Dog Blue** – Characteristics of honeydew and apricot highlight this semisweet, Riesling blend.

◆ **Cabernet Franc** – This wine has blackberry jam, vanilla, and oak aromas. It is aged primarily in American oak and blended with wine that is aged in French oak.

◆ **Pinot Noir** – This is a light, red wine with rich cedar and cherry aromas. Made from a mix of Pinot grapes that are fermented separately, it is blended with a small amount of Cabernet Franc for balance.

◆ **Chardonnay** – This well-rounded dry wine has apple, pineapple, and buttery aromas.

◆ **Merlot** – This medium body dry red wine is accented by blackberry jam with a hint of mint and Eucalyptus.

CHRYSALIS VINEYARDS

◆ **Mariposa** – This is a full-bodied and bold dry wine, and its bright pink color foretells its fruity character. It offers fragrant aromas and flavors that hint at raspberry, melon, and cherry.

COOPER VINEYARDS

◆ **Norton** – This is a saturated and intense mix of bold flavors with an elegant silky finish. It is aged in both Virginia and French oak barrels for 10 months.

◆ **Chardonnay** – This is a harmonious blend of fruit from two separate vineyards. A citrus nose leads into honey rich fruit flavors followed by a creamy vanilla finish.

◆ **Coopertage Blanc** – This wine is a blend of Viognier and Chardonnay.

◆ **Sweet Louisa** – A blend of 70 percent Munsen and 30 percent Chardonnay is Concord-like in flavor with 5 percent residual sugar.

FARFELU VINEYARDS

◆ **Fou de Rouge** – This is a light, red wine with notes of cherry and spice.

◆ **Riesling** – Made from hand-selected fully ripened grapes, this wine has delicate floral and peach flavors, soft texture and a crisp lemon acidity.

FIRST COLONY WINERY

◆ **Blush** – This wine is a blend of Cabernet Franc and Vidal Blanc. The nose exhibits hints of strawberry and the mouth is slightly sweet.

◆ **Cabernet Franc** – This Beaujolais-style Cabernet Franc exhibits intense fruit on the nose and mouth. It has a hint of oak and a spicy, peppery finish.

◆ **Vidal Blanc** – This wonderful, dry wine has aromas of apple and pear, an abundance of citrus fruit on the palate, and a crisp dry finish.

GABRIELE RAUSSE WINERY

◆ *Cabernet Sauvignon* – Earth, tar, and leather notes are evident in this Cabernet with modest fruit and high acidity.

HARTWOOD WINERY

◆ *Rappahannock Rose* – This traditionally styled rose wine is dry and made from a blend of Chambourcin and Seyval Blanc. Soft cherry-like flavors are balanced by hints of citrus.

HORTON CELLARS WINERY

◆ *Cotes d' Orange* – This complex, rich, and fruity wine is enhanced with pepper spice, smoke, and leather flavors.
◆ *Norton* – This wine has rich aromas of plum and cherries with a long, spicy finish.
◆ *Petit Manseng* – This wine has an engaging Pina Colada nose. It is rich with creamy flavors followed by a clean and firm acidic backbone.
◆ *Spotswood Trail Chardonnay* – Smokey, buttery aromas are followed by a full-bodied wine with a very long, spicy finish. It is 100 percent fermented and aged in French oak.
◆ *Stonecastle White* – This fine blend of Viognier, Marsanne and Chardonnay has a floral nose, rich fruit, and a semi-sweet finish.

INGLESIDE PLANTATION VINEYARDS

◆ *Brut Sparkling Wine* – This delicately textured Methode Champenoise has a crisp mouth feel and a touch of sweetness.
◆ *Colonial Rose* – This is a medium-bodied wine with hints of licorice and cherry. This wine has a rich, sweet finish.
◆ *Blue Crab Red Wine* – This semi-dry wine has spice and fruit in the bouquet that give way to a soft, slightly sweet finish.
◆ *Chardonnay* – This is a classic Chardonnay with lingering pear and vanilla flavors and an oak finish.
◆ *Pinot Gris* – This is a dry wine with delicate hints of citrus.

JEFFERSON VINEYARDS

◆ *Merlot* – Aged for a year in French and American oak barrels, this wine has spicy and peppery notes. The bright, red fruit flavors round out the palate of this extremely smooth vintage.
◆ *Chardonnay Reserve* – This wine is dry and full-bodied with intense flavors. This blend of the best grapes is 100 percent fermented and aged in French oak barrels.

KING FAMILY VINEYARDS

◆ *Chardonnay* – Barrel-fermented and sur lies aged in French oak, this Chardonnay has 100 percent malolactic fermentation. It has a buttery taste with vanilla aromas and pear and ripe apple notes.
◆ *Loreley Late Harvest Viognier* – The aromas of this Viognier are filled with candied fruit notes of apricots and pears. The palate is rich and dense with a lingering finish.
◆ *Michael Shaps Viognier* – This is a rich, flavorful wine with aromatic qualities. The bouquet is mostly apricot with hints of baked pineapple and toasted oak aromas.

KLUGE ESTATE WINERY & VINEYARD

◆ *Kluge Estate SP* – This is the first sparkling white wine from Kluge Estate. Made with Chardonnay grapes in the traditional method Champenoise style, it is a classical French blanc de blanc. Loaded with tiny, effervescent bubbles, SP is an energetic brut.
◆ *New World Red* – This Bordeaux-style blend is made from Cabernet Sauvignon, Merlot, and Cabernet Franc. It is smooth, round, and soft with notes characterized by toasted oak, currant, and black cherry. The finish delivers a flourish of mocha and coffee.

LAKE ANNA WINERY

◆ *Chardonnay* – This Chardonnay invokes flavors of heirloom apples with toasted almonds and brown spices.
◆ *Lake Side White* – This is a semi-dry wine with flavors of dried peaches and vanilla and a touch of lime zest.

LA PROVENCALE CELLARS

◆ *Le Mousseux Sparkling Virginia Cider* – Le Mousseux translates roughly as "the bubbles." This sparkling cider is made from the natural unfermented juice of a hand-selected blend of fresh apples grown in Virginia's apple country in the Shenandoah Valley. The cuvee—a blend of several varieties chosen for flavor, acidity, and aroma—includes Macintosh for sweet fruit flavor and Jonathan for aromatic intensity. It has a sophisticated dry apple aroma with a spicy flavor and a crisp finish.

LINDEN VINEYARDS

◆ *Seyval* – This wine exhibits aromas of fresh spring flowers and lime zest. Flavors are very dry, grapefruity, and crisp.
◆ *Riesling Vidal* – This wine has a crisp acidity and a bit of sweetness. It contains aromas of tropical fruit, especially pineapple, as well as some peach and apricot.

LOUDOUN VALLEY VINEYARDS

◆ *Vinifera White* – This is a blend of barrel-fermented Chardonnay and Riesling. A dry wine with flavors of rich spiciness and a balance of fruit and oak.

MOBJACK BAY BEER COMPANY

◆ *Pale Ale* – This classic American pale ale is brewed with four different malts and generous additions of Cascade and Willamette hops, making it a crisp and flavorful beer.

NAKED MOUNTAIN VINEYARD

◆ *Chardonnay* – This is a crisp, dry white wine with pronounced Chardonnay fruit in the nose. The primary palate flavors are those of toasty vanilla, butterscotch, ripe fig, and anise. Balancing out the wine are the more subtle flavors of nutmeg, ginger, and citrus. It also invokes fruit flavors such as pineapple, grapefruit, apple, peach, pear, and melon—with a kiss of oak.

NORTH MOUNTAIN VINEYARD & WINERY

◆ *Chambourcin* – This is a full-bodied red wine made in the traditional manner, using the varietal grape Chambourcin. It is round in the mouth with a softness that evokes a Merlot.
◆ *Chardonnay* – This dry, full-flavored wine is barrel fermented in oak.
◆ *Riesling* – This crisp, blended white wine has hints of citrus.
◆ *Vidal Blanc* – This is a fruity, fabulous picnic wine filled with crisp citrus flavors and a fresh flowery bouquet.

OAKENCROFT VINEYARD & WINERY

◆ *NV Sweet Virginia* – This blend of Seyval Blanc and Vidal Blanc has a little Muscat for sweetness. Fermented cold in stainless steel, this wine has a beautiful honeysuckle nose.
◆ *Countryside Red* – This is a fresh, fruity, semi-dry wine blended from 70 percent Chambourcin, 20 percent Cabernet Sauvignon, and 10 percent Merlot.
◆ *Chardonnay* – This Chardonnay is nicely balanced with a hint of oak. Fermented primarily in stainless steel, it has plenty of crisp citrus flavors.
◆ *VC Classic* – This is an exciting blend of 80 percent Viognier and 20 percent barrel-fermented Chardonnay. It has nice, floral notes with a full, round finish.

OASIS WINERY

◆ *Brut* – A sparkling wine with nutty, pear, and fresh-cut apple aromas. Very smooth with small delicate spiraling bubbles.
◆ *Reserve Cabernet Sauvignon* – This Bordeaux-style red wine is made from the oldest vines in Virginia. Touches of Merlot and Cabernet Franc are blended into this Cabernet Sauvignon. Extended skin contact makes this an intense, yet soft and dry, red wine.
◆ *Barrel Select Chardonnay* – Fermented to dryness in new French oak, this wine was made from some of the oldest plantings in Virginia in the manner of a White Burgundy. This wine explodes with vanilla and buttery characters with a fresh citrus varietal bouquet.
◆ *Riesling* – This 100 percent Johannesburg Riesling is semi-dry and fermented in stainless steel.

OLD HOUSE VINEYARDS

◆ *Merlot* – Plum and wild cherry aromas blend with the oak flavors to add life to this rich, red wine. Bold fruit flavors in the mouth with a soft, lingering finish.

PRINCE MICHEL & RAPIDAN RIVER VINEYARDS

◆ *Madison Reserve Rose* – This wine has aromas of ripe strawberries and apricot. It is slightly sweet with an elegant balance.
◆ *The Prince's Virginia Brut Sparkling Wine* – 100 percent Pinot Noir, this wine exhibits classic fruit and toasty, yeasty characteristics.
◆ *Gewurztraminer* – This dry wine has fruity and spicy characteristics.
◆ *Rapidan River Dry Riesling* – This wine has aromas of apricot, mango, and rose petal. It is full flavored with a crisp and delightful blend.

REBEC VINEYARDS

◆ *Gewurztraminer* – This is a naturally spicy wine bursting with intense fruit.
◆ *Viognier* – This dry white Rhone wine has a distinctive bouquet of apricots and spring flowers.

ROCKBRIDGE VINEYARD

◆ *DeChiel Pinot Noir* – This elegant, light-bodied red has fragrant cherry fruit and a hint of black pepper.
◆ *Tuscarora White* – This is a fruity, semi-dry blend based on the Vidal Blanc grape with crisp acidity.
◆ *White Riesling* – This is a refreshing and fruity, semi-dry wine with a hint of spice and sweetness.

ST. GEORGE BREWERY

◆ *Golden Ale* – This ale is based on an old British recipe but with an American twist – a slightly sweet, malty flavor with a citrus finish. It has a thick, creamy head and is golden amber in color.
◆ *Pilsner* – This is a clean, crisp lager. A centuries-old conditioning process and a unique lager yeast result in this exceptionally smooth beer. Traditional 2 Row Pale and Munich Malts along with noble German Hops ensure a well-balanced, pale golden lager with a fine creamy head.
◆ *Porter* – A complex tapestry of flavors in a ruby black ale with a rich malt base, results in caramel and chocolate tones, classically balanced with English bitters and aromatic hops.

STONE MOUNTAIN VINEYARDS

◆ *Chardonnay* – Stainless steel fermentation produces luscious ripeness and a crisp lingering finish. Orange blossom honey, perfectly ripe green apple, pineapple, and other tropical fruits dominate the bouquet.

STONEWALL VINEYARDS & WINERY

◆ *Chambourcin* – Light and dry from nonskin fermentation and light oak aging, this red wine is low in tannins.

◆ *Vidal Blanc* – A crisp, dry white wine lightly aged in oak barrels with a hint of citrus on the finish.

TARARA VINEYARD & WINERY

◆ *Meritage* – This classic Bordeaux-style red is a blend from the reserve lots of Cabernet Sauvignon, Merlot, and Cabernet Franc and is aged for 18 months in oak barrels.

◆ *Charvel* – This lighter-styled white wine is a blend of Chardonnay and Seyval Blanc. The stainless steel fermentation process creates a fruity and floral wine.

UNICORN WINERY

◆ *Chambourcin* – This wine has a dark, inky color with a black cherry nose. A full range of flavors from upfront plum and berry fruit to smoky tobacco and anise meld on the palate and are woven in a burgundy structure.

◆ *Seyvral* – This white wine is dry, crisp, and fruity.

VALHALLA VINEYARDS

◆ *Dry Rose* – This wine blends 50 percent Sangiovese and 50 percent Cabernet Franc. After 48 hours of cold soaking, the saignee is drawn off and vinified separately in neutral French oak barrels and aged for nine months before bottling. This wine abounds with strawberry fruit on the nose and palate, refreshing and crisp.

◆ *Sangiovese* – Made from the same grape as Chianti, this wine is loaded with aromas and flavors of strawberry, cherry, and a hint of spice.

◆ *Syrah* – This wine is big and bold with a fruit and pepper nose. Flavors of chocolate, fresh berries, and cocoa coat the palate.

◆ *Chardonnay* – Cold pressed and fermented in French oak, this wine has aromas of ripe citrus and toasty oak with a good, long finish.

VILLA APPALACCIA WINERY

◆ *Pinot Grigio* – This crisp, fresh white wine has hints of grapefruit, pears, and green apples.

WHITE HALL VINEYARDS

◆ *Cabernet Sauvignon* – Deep extraction of ripe, dark fruit results in a concentrated nose of black cherry and cassis, followed by generous anise and spice on the palate.

◆ *Gewurztraminer* – Subdued mango and pear aromas awaken the palate, leading to a lovely bouquet of cinnamon, lychee fruit, and a crisp apple flare.

◆ *Merlot* – This wine has an attractive nose of red fruits, minty herbs, and mocha notes with a palate showing smooth and supple red currants, wild cherries, cocoa, and soft ripe tannins.

WILLIAMSBURG BREWING COMPANY

◆ *Pale Ale*™ – This classic American-style ale has a very full, but well-balanced, hop profile.

◆ *Porter*™ – This is a dark brown ale with a deep, complex, robust style.

◆ *Wheat Ale*™ – This is a light wheat ale with a refreshing, unfiltered American style.

THE WILLIAMSBURG WINERY

◆ *Burgesses' Measure Merlot* – A medium-bodied red varietal, the wine is light in tannins with a taste reminiscent of raspberries. It is well-balanced with fruit and oak and is aged in French and American barrels.

◆ *Two Shilling Red* – This is a medium-bodied blend with aromas that are fresh and slightly floral.

◆ *Acte 12 Chardonnay* – Harmonious and smooth, this wine is designed to exhibit the soft, toasty character of French oak barrels without overwhelming its fruit structure.

◆ *Governor's White* – This white table wine is a fresh, fruity, semi-dry blend with a good sugar and acid balance. Peach and herbal flavors are exhibited in the nose.

WINTERGREEN WINERY

◆ *Raspberry* – This dessert-style fruit wine has a bold, fresh raspberry taste.

◆ *Black Rock Chardonnay Reserve* – This dry and full-bodied Chardonnay has tropical fruit notes and a supple, creamy palate.

◆ *Chardonnay Monticello* – This wine is fermented cool to produce a dry, crisp wine with distinct tropical and citrus notes. It is well-balanced with pleasing acidity.

◆ *Riesling* – This wine is fruity and floral with a spicy finish and a healthy acidity.

Virginia Wine History

At the inception of the Jamestown colony in 1607, English settlers were already thinking of producing wine in their new land. The wine was not just for their consumption but for the overseas market as well; it was commonly known that high profits could be expected for successful winemakers. In 1609, the first wine was produced from native grapes; however, it was not as successful as the settlers had hoped. Over the next two years the settlers saw frustrating and unsuccessful attempts to produce a palatable wine. In 1611, eager to launch winemaking in the new colony, vineyard specialists arrived from England to aid the settlers.

In 1624, a requirement by the House mandated that 20 vines be planted for each male colonist above age 20. French viticulturists were brought to the New World; however, they too failed to transplant European viticulture. On the eve of the American Revolution in 1769, the Virginia Assembly appointed Andrew Estave, a French vineyardist, as winemaker and viticulturist for their new colony. Just like all those who tried before him to produce wine in the New World, Estave failed.

Although he failed at producing wine, Estave made an important discovery concerning the grapes that were being planted. Estave concluded that the European vitus vinifera grapes were too fragile for the American climate and that only native American grapes would flourish in the Virginia climate, which consisted of cold winters and hot, humid summers. By the turn of the century, Estave's conclusion was widely accepted and would initiate development of the strong wine industry currently found in Virginia.

Thomas Jefferson, credited as being the father of American wine, was anxious to see winemaking develop in America. Jefferson saw its pleasing qualities and envisioned wine as an alternative crop that could lessen the colony's dependence on tobacco, which was, at that time, the number one cash crop in Virginia. In 1773, Jefferson gave 2,000 acres of land to Philip Mazzei, who also believed native American grapes were the foundation of successful winemaking, with the hope that Mazzei could successfully produce Virginia wine.

Mazzei's efforts at winemaking were interrupted by the Revolutionary War and never resumed. The war, however, did not deter Jefferson as he continued to cultivate his knowledge and love of wines. Jefferson served as an Ambassador to France, where he closely studied the winemaking areas of Europe. He returned home to America an even more enthusiastic ambassador of wines, encouraging all Americans to drink wine with their meals. He became a wine advisor to several American presidents and, at the request of America's first President George Washington, Jefferson selected wines to be stocked in the White House.

Jefferson believed that wine was a healthier beverage choice than harder spirits; a theory that is supported today by many modern medical studies. Jefferson once commented, "In countries which use ardent spirits, drunkenness is the mortal vice; but in those countries which make wine for common use, you never see a drunkard."

Jefferson loved European wines; however, he, too, agreed with Mazzei and Sestave that to create a successful American winemaking industry, native American grapes must be used. They weren't the only ones who thought this way and, by 1800, other Virginians started developing hybrids of American and European varieties. These hybrids resulted in grapes that combined American hardiness with European finesse and complexity. The most popular were the Alexander, Norton, Catawba, Isabella, Niagara, Concord, and Delaware, all of which are still grown today.

In the years following 1800 before the outbreak of the War Between the States, a strong winemaking industry developed in Virginia. As a result of the many devastating battles fought in the state during the war, vineyards were destroyed along with the economy. This left Virginia winemakers unable to compete with wines produced elsewhere, especially those being grown in California. In the late 1800s, Virginia began prohibiting alcohol, stunting the winemaking industry. By 1914, when Virginia voted to legally prohibit alcohol, few vineyards remained in the state. By 1950, there were only 15 acres of grapes grown in the state, most for table consumption.

During the 1960's, the grape industry in Virginia began a revival, beginning with American hybrids. An increasing appetite for wine fueled the comeback of Virginia grapes and wines. The market for wine already existed in metropolitan areas and local farmers were receptive to grapes as an alternative crop. These factors, combined with favorable growing conditions, began a new era of winemaking across Virginia.

By the 1970s, the emphasis shifted to French hybrids. In the early 1970s, Virginia began cultivating vinifera varietals, a grape appealing to sophisticated palates. By 1982, vinifera varietals became the preference of Virginia grape growers, producing what have become the most popular Virginia wines: Chardonnay, Riesling, and Cabernet Sauvignon. Merlot is another vinifera varietal that is growing in popularity. The most popular French hybrids are Seyval and Vidal. Other varietals are gaining attractiveness as demand for Virginia wines grows along with the state's ability to produce successful wines.

Crucial to the tremendous growth of the Virginia wine industry is the favorable climate illustrated by the Farm Winery Law of 1980. A notable provision of the law is that, to qualify as a farm winery, at least 51 percent of its wine must come from grapes owned or leased by the winery. A benefit of this provision is that wineries do not need more than one license to sell wine at both the wholesale and retail levels. Additional support came during the 1980s when both the state and the United States Department of Agriculture began programs through Virginia Tech to assist in the growing of Virginia wine grapes to improve palatability. Virginia Tech's efforts have greatly improved the Virginia wine industry and helped stabilize individual wineries.

Additionally, the Virginia Wine Marketing Board, in conjunction with the Virginia Department of Agriculture and Consumer Services, help support the wine industry. At present, Virginia wines have won both national and international acclaim. To truly appreciate this achievement, it is important to remember that Virginia didn't have a wine industry until the 1970s. The success of Virginia wines can also be attributed to knowledge gained about weather and local conditions, allowing vineyardists to develop tough strains that are able to thrive in the varying and challenging Virginia climate.

Grape variations that range from the Blue Ridge to the Eastern Shore produce variable vintages that have sensory differences in both taste and flavor, increasing the appeal of Virginia wines. The recognizable differences of wines from different regions aid Virginia's tourism industry, bringing visitors to wineries and festivals across the Commonwealth. More than 350 years have passed since the Jamestown colonists first attempted to establish a successful wine industry in Virginia. Finally, their blood, sweat, and tears have come to fruition as wineries flourish across the state of Virginia. Assuredly all those who tried yieldlessly to establish the wine industry would today be proud, perhaps amazed, at how Virginia wines are growing in appeal and recognition throughout the nation and the world.

Sources:
Virginia Wines Web site at http://www.virginiawines.org/about/history2.html, reviewed April 2004.
Geocities Web site at http://www.geocities.com/Wellesley/Garden/1077/vawinehistory.html, reviewed April 2004.

Source Guide

Abingdon Vineyard & Winery
20530 Alvarado Road
Abingdon, VA 24211
(276) 623-1255
www.abingdonwinery.com
info@abingdonwinery.com

Afton Mountain Vineyards
234 Vineyard Lane
Afton, VA 22920
(540) 456-8667
Fax: (540) 456-8002
corpora@cfw.com

AmRhein Wine Cellars
9243 Patterson Drive
Bent Mountain, VA 24059
(540) 929-4632
Fax: (540) 929-4632
www.roanokewine.com
jackieamrhein@att.net

**Autumn Hill Vineyards/
Blue Ridge Winery**
301 River Drive
Stanardsville, VA 22973
(434) 985-6100
Fax: (434) 985-3081
www.autumnhillwine.com
autumnhill@mindspring.com

Barboursville Vineyards
Rt. 777, Box 136
Barboursville, VA 22923
(540) 832-3824
Fax: (540) 832-7572
www.barboursvillewine.com
bvvy@baboursvillewine.com

Blenheim Vineyards
31 Blenheim Farm
Charlottesville, VA 22903
(434) 293-5366
Fax: (434) 293-5524
www.blenheimvineyards.com
brad@blenheimvineyards.com

Bloxon Vineyard & Winery
26130 Mason Road
Bloxom, VA 23308-2639
(757) 665-5670
Fax: (757) 665-5670
casablancawine@ICQmail.com

Blue Crab Bay Company
29368 Atlantic Drive
Melfa, VA 23410
(757) 787-3602
(800) 221-2722
Fax: (757) 787-3430
www.bluecrabbay.com
sales@bluecrabbay.com
*Sharing the tastes and traditions of the
Chesapeake Bay region.*

Boundary Rock Farm & Vineyard
414 Riggins Road
Willis, VA 24380
(540) 789-7098
www.boundaryrock.com
boundaryrock@yahoo.com

**Bowman's™ Virginia Vodka
A. Smith Distillery**
Fredericksburg, VA 22408

Breaux Vineyards
36888 Breaux Vineyards Lane
Purcellville, VA 20132
(540) 668-6299
Fax: (540) 668-6283
www.breauxvineyards.com
Breauxvin@aol.com

**Burnley Vineyards
& Daniel Cellars**
4500 Winery Lane
Barboursville, VA 22923
(540) 832-2828
Fax: (540) 832-2280
www.burnleywines.com
burnleywines@rlc.net

**Cardinal Point Vineyard
& Winery**
9423 Batesville Road
Afton VA 22920
(540) 456-8400
Fax: (540) 456-8400
www.cardinalpointwinery.com
contact@cardinalpointwinery.com

Chateau Morrisette
287 Winery Road
Floyd, VA 24091
(540) 593-2865
Fax: (540) 593-2868
www.thedogs.com
info@thedogs.com

Christensen Ridge
HCR 02, Box 459
Madison, VA 22727
(540) 923-4800
Fax: (540) 923-4900
www.christensenridge.com
info@christensenridge.com; lodg-
ing@christensenridge.com

Chrysalis Vineyards
23876 Champe Ford Road
Middleburg, VA 20117
(540) 687-8222
(800) 235-8804
Fax: (540) 687-8666
www.chrysaliswine.com
info@chrysaliswine.com

Cooper Vineyards
13372 Shannon Hill Road
Louisa, VA 23093
(540) 894-5253
Fax: (804) 285-8773
www.coopervineyards.com
gcooper@erols.com
jphogge@msn.com

Davis Valley Winery & Vineyard
Box KK
Saltville VA 24370
(276) 492-6928
rustydsm@aol.com

Deer Meadow Vineyard
199 Vintage Lane
Winchester, VA 22602
(540) 877-1919
(800) 653-6632
dmeadow@shentel.net

Dominion Wine Cellars
1 Winery Avenue, P.O. Box 1057
Culpeper, VA 22701
(540) 825-8772
Fax: (540) 829-0377
www.williamsburgwineryltd.com
dsampson@wmbgwine.com

Dye's Vineyard
RR2, Box 357
Honaker, VA 24260
(276) 873-4659
www.dyesvineyards.com
cleodye@yahoo.com

Farfelu Vineyards
13058 Crest Hill Road
Flint Hill, VA 22627
(540) 364-2930
Fax: (540) 364-3930
www.farfeluwine.com
c-osborne@farfeluwine.com

Farm Fresh Supermarkets
853 Chimney Hill Shopping Center
Virginia Beach, VA 23452
(757) 306-2090
Fax: (757) 306-2282
www.farmfreshmarkets.com
susan.t.mayo@supervalu.com
*Farm Fresh Supermarkets-When Only
The Very Best Will Do!**

Fincastle Vineyard & Winery
203 Maple Ridge Lane
Fincastle, VA 24090
(540) 591-9000
www.fincastlewine.com
fincastlewine@yahoo.com

First Colony Winery
1650 Harris Creek Road
Charlottesville, VA 22902
(434) 979-7105
Fax: (434) 293-2054
www.firstcolonywinery.com
firstcolonywinery@earthlink.net

Garbriele Rausse Winery
P.O. Box 3956
Charlottesville, VA 22903
(434) 296-5328
Fax: (434) 296-5328

Gray Ghost Vineyards
14706 Lee Highway
Amissville, VA 20106-4226
(540) 937-4869
Fax: (540) 937-4869

Grayhaven Winery
4675 East Grey Fox Circle
Gum Spring, VA 23065
(804) 556-3917
www.grayhavenwinery.com
max@grayhavenwinery.com

Source Guide continued

Guilford Ridge Vineyard
328 Running Pine Road
Luray, VA 22835
(540) 778-3853

Hampton Roads Magazine
1264 Perimeter Parkway
Virginia Beach, VA 23454
Phone: (757) 422-8979
Fax: (757) 422-9092
www.hamptonroadsmagazine.com
george@hrmag.com
Hampton Roads Magazine-The city and lifestyle magazine of Hampton Roads!

Hartwood Winery
345 Hartwood Road
Fredericksburg, VA 22406
(540) 752-4893
Fax: (540) 752-4893
jdliving@erols.com

Hickory Hill Vineyard
1722 Hickory Cove Lane
Moneta, VA 24121
(540) 296-1393
www.hickoryhillvineyards.com
info@hickoryhillvineyards.com

Hidden Brook Winery
43301 Spinks Ferry Road
Leesburg, VA 20176
(703) 737-3935
www.hiddenbrookwinery.com
hiddenbrookwine@aol.com

Highlands Harvest Vineyard and Farm Winery
Route 2, Box 321
Castlewood, VA 24224
(276) 762-7546
Fax: (276) 762-9561
buffalo@cablenet-va.com

Hill Top Berry Farm & Winery
2800 Berry Hill Road
Nellysford, VA 22958
(434) 361-1266
Fax: (434) 361-1266
hilltop1@intelos.net

Hillsborough Vineyards
36716 Charles Town PK
Purcellville, VA 20132
(540) 668-7787

Horton Cellars Winery
6399 Spotswood Trail
Gordonsville, VA 22942
(540) 832-7440
Fax: (540) 832-7187
www.hvwine.com
vawinee@aol.com

House of Marquis, Ltd.
1017 Thomas Jefferson Parkway
Charlottesville, VA 22902
(434) 979-2965
Fax: (434) 244-0090

Hubbard Peanut Company, Inc.
P.O. Box 94
Sedley, VA 23878
(800) 889-7688
(757) 562-4081
Fax: (757) 562-2741
www.hubspeanuts.com
hubs@hubspeanuts.com
They're not just peanuts, they're Hubs: The best of Virginia, cooked to perfection!

Hummel Vineyards
1005 Panorama Road
Montross, VA 22520
(804) 493-1544
Fax: (804) 493-0747
panorama@rivnet.net

Ingleside Plantation Vineyards
5872 Leedstown Road
Oak Grove, VA 22443
(804) 224-8687
Fax: (804) 224-8573
www.ipwine.com
mail@ipwine.com

James River Cellars
11008 Washington Highway
Glen Allen, VA 23059
(804) 550-7516
Fax: (804) 550-1869
www.jamesrivercellars.com
winecellars@jrgm.com

Jefferson Vineyards
1353 Thomas Jefferson Parkway
Charlottesville, VA 22902
(434) 977-3042
Fax: (434) 977-5459
www.jeffersonvineyards.com
info@jeffersonvineyards.com

Keswick Vineyards
1575 Keswick Winery Drive
Keswick, VA 22947
(434) 244-3341
Fax: (434) 244-9976
www.keswickvineyards.com
info@keswickvineyards.com

King Family Vineyards/ Michael Shaps Wines
6550 Roseland Farm
Crozet, VA 22932
(434) 823-7800
Fax: (434) 823-7801
www.kingfamilyvineyards.com
info@kingfamilyvineyards.com

The Kluge Estate Winery and Vineyard
100 Grand Cru Drive
Charlottesville, VA 22902
(434) 977-3895
Fax: (434) 977-0606
www.klugeestate.com
info@klugeestate.com

La Provencale Cellars Le Mousseux Sparkling Cider
PO Box 41117
Fredericksburg, VA 22404
www.lemousseux.com
cider@laprovencalecellars.com

Lake Anna Winery
5621 Courthouse Road
Spotsylvania, VA 22553
(540) 895-5085
Fax: (540) 895-9749
www.lawinery.com
LakeAnnaWinery@cs.com

Landwirt Vineyard
8223 Simmers Valley Road
Harrisonburg, VA 22802
(540) 833-6000
Fax: (540) 833-6006
www.valleyva.com/landwirt.html
landwirt@shentel.net

Linden Beverage Company Alpenglow Sparkling Cider
4275 John Marshall Highway
Linden, VA 22642
(540) 635-2118
www.alpenglow.net

Linden Vineyards
3708 Harrels Corner Road
Linden, VA 22642
(540) 364-1997
Fax: (540) 364-3894
www.lindenvineyards.com
linden@crosslink.net

Lost Creek Winery
43227 Spinks Ferry Road
Leesburg, VA 20176
(703) 443-9836
Fax: (703) 406-9815
www.lostcreekwinery.com
winery@lostcreek.com

Loudoun Valley Vineyards
38516 Charlestown Pike
Waterford, VA 20197
(540) 882-3375
www.loudounvalleyvineyards.com
wine@loudounvalleyvineyards.com

Mobjack Bay Beer Company
(804) 330-4665
www.mobjack.net

Mountain Cove Vineyards and Winegarden
1362 Fortunes Cove Lane
Lovingston, VA 22949
(434) 263-5392
Fax: (434) 263-8540
aweed1@juno.com

Naked Mountain Vineyard
2747 Leeds Manor Road
Markham, VA 22643
(540) 364-1609
Fax: (540) 364-4870
www.nakedmtn.com
pgharper@erols.com
nakedmountain@yahoo.com

North Mountain Vineyard & Winery
4374 Swartz Road
Maurertown, VA 22644
(540) 436-9463
www.northmountainvineyard.com
wine@northmountainvineyard.com

Source Guide continued

Oak Crest Vineyard & Winery
8215 Oak Crest Drive
King George, VA 22485
(540) 663-2813
oakcrest@crosslink.net

Oakencroft Vineyard & Winery
1486 Oakencroft Lane
Charlottesville, VA 22901
(434) 296-4188
Fax: (434) 293-6631
www.oakencroft.com
mail@oakencroft.com

Oasis Winery
Rt. 635, 14141 Hume Road
Hume, VA 22639
(540) 635-7627
(800) 304-7656
Fax: (540) 635-4653
www.oasiswine.com
oasiswine@aol.com

Old House Vineyards
18351 Corky's Lane
Culpeper, VA 22701
(540) 423-1032
Fax: (703) 938-2744
www.oldhousevineyards.com
info@oldhouse.com

Peaks of Otter Winery
2122 Sheep Creek Road
Bedford, VA 24523
(540) 586-3707
www.peaksofotterwinery.com
appleseed@earthlink.net

Pearmund Cellars
6109 Georgetown Road
Broad Run, VA 20137
(540) 347-3475
Fax: (540) 349-9791
chris@pearmundcellars.com

Piedmont Vineyards and Winery
P.O. Box 286,
Route 626 South
Middleburg, VA 20118
(540) 687-5528
Fax: (540) 687-5777
www.piedmontwines.com
info@piedmontwines.com

Pinnacle Network Systems, Inc.
P O Box 64785
Virginia Beach, VA 23467
(757) 449-3774
Fax: (757) 490-0466
www.pnsys.com
jim.peele@pnsys.com
"Vision provides direction, planning provides a roadmap, and PEOPLE get you there"

Prince Michel & Rapidan River Vineyards
154 Winery Lane
Leon, VA 22725
(800) 800-WINE
(suites & restaurant)
Fax: (540) 547-3088
www.princemichel.com
info@princemichel.com

Rappahannock Cellars
14437 Hume Road
Huntly, VA 22640
(540) 635-9398
www.rappahannockcellars.com
winery@rappahanockcellars.com

Rebec Vineyards
2229 North Amherst Highway
Amherst, VA 24521
(434) 946-5168
Fax: (434) 946-5168
www.rebecwinery.com
winery@rebecwinery.com

Rockbridge Vineyard
30 Hill View Lane
Raphine, VA 24472
(540) 377-6204
(888) 511-WINE
Fax: (540) 377-6204
www.rockbridgewine.com
rocwine@cfw.com

Rogers Ford Farm Winery
14674 Rogers Ford Road
Sumerduck, VA 22742
(540) 439-3707
Fax: (540) 439-3757
www.rogersfordwine.com
johnpuckett@earthlink.net

Rose River Vineyards & Trout Farm
Route 648 Box 186
Syria, VA 22743
(540) 923-4050
www.roseriverwine.com
ken@roseriverwine.com

San-J International, Inc.
2880 Sprouse Drive
Richmond, VA 23231
(804) 226-8333
(804) 226-8383
www.san-j.com
sales@san-j.com
"Celebrating 200 years of premium Tamari soy sauce—Taste the Tamari Difference"

Sharp Rock Vineyards
5 Sharp Rock Road
Sperryville, VA 22740
(540) 987-9700
Fax: (540) 987-9031
www.sharprock.com
darmor@sharprock.com

Shenandoah Vineyards, Inc.
3659 South Ox Road
Edinburg, VA 22824
(540) 984-8699
Fax: (540) 984-9463
www.shentel.net/shenvine
shenvine@shentel.net

Smithfield
501 North Church Street
Smithfield, VA 23430
(757) 357-4321
Fax: (757) 357-1650
www.smithfield.com
Mail Orders: 1-800-926-8448
Smithfield, where eating well has a rich tradition.

Smokehouse Winery
10 Ashby Road
Sperryville, VA 22740
(540) 987-3194
Fax: (540) 987-8189
www.smokehousewinerybnb.com
smokehouse@tidalwave.net

Spotted Tavern Winery/ Dodd's Cider Mill
P.O. Box 175
Hartwood, VA 22471
(540) 752-4453
Fax: (540) 752-4611

Stillhouse Vineyards
4366 Stillhouse Road
Hume, VA 22639
(540) 364-1203
www.stillhousevineyards.com
John@stillhousevineyards.com

Stone Mountain Vineyards
1376 Wyatt Mountain Road
Dyke, VA 22935
(434) 990-WINE
www.stonemountainvineyards.com
info@stonemountainvineyards.com

Stonewall Vineyards & Winery
Route 2 Box 107 A
Concord, VA 24538
(434) 993-2185
Fax: (434) 993-3875
www.stonewallwine.com
stonewallwine@juno.com

St. George Brewing
204 Challenger Way
Hampton, VA 23666
(757) 865-7781
arathmann@stgeorgebrewingco.com

Swedenburg Estate Vineyard
23595 Winery Lane
Middleburg, VA 20117-2847
(540) 687-5219
www.swedenburgwines.com

Tarara Vineyard & Winery
13648 Tarara Lane
Leesburg, VA 20176
(703) 771-7100
Metro DC: (703) 478-8161
Fax: (703) 771-8443
www.tarara.com
marta.wallace@tarara.com

Source Guide continued

Tomahawk Mill Winery
9221 Anderson Mill Road
Chatham, VA 24531
(434) 432-4063
Fax: (434) 432-2037
www.tomahawkmill.com
Tomahawk@gamewood.net

Unicorn Winery
487 Old Bridge Road
Amissville, VA 20106
(540) 349-5885
www.unicornwinery.com
info@unicornwinery.com

**United Way
of South Hampton Roads**
2515 Walmer Avenue
Norfolk, VA 23541
Phone; (757) 853-8500
Fax: (757) 853-3900
www.unitedwayshr.org
*United Way
of South Hampton Roads
supports our youth in building a better
community*

Valhalla Vineyards
6500 Mt. Chestnut Road
Roanoke, VA 24018
(540) 725-WINE (9463)
Fax: (540) 772-7858
www.valhallawines.com
info@valhallawines.com

Veramar Vineyard
905 Quarry Road
Berryville, VA 22611
(540) 955-5510
Fax: (540) 955-0404
www.veramar.com
veramar1@msn.com

Veritas Winery
145 Saddleback Farm
Afton, VA 22920
(540) 456-8000
Fax: (540) 456-8483
www.veritaswines.com
veritasvineyards@aol.com

Villa Appalaccia Winery
753 Rock Castle Gorge
Floyd, VA 24091
(540) 593-3100
(919) 966-3015
www.villaappalaccia.com
chianti@villaappalaccia.com

**Virginia Gouda Cheese
Monastery Country Cheese
Our Lady of the Angels Monastery**
3365 Monastery Dr
Crozet, VA 22932
(434) 823-1452

White Hall Vineyards
5190 Sugar Ridge Road
White Hall, VA 22987
(434) 823-8615
Fax: (434) 823-4366
www.whitehallvineyards.com
tastingroom@
whitehallvineyards.com

Williamsburg Brewing Company
189-B Ewell Road
Williamsburg, VA 23188
(757) 253-1577
www.williamsburgbrewing.com

The Williamsburg Winery, Ltd.
5800 Wessex Hundred
Williamsburg, VA 23185-8063
(757) 229-0999
Fax: (757) 229-0911
www.williamsburgwinery.com
wine@wmbgwine.com

Willowcroft Farm Vineyards
38906 Mount Gilead Road
Leesburg, VA 20175
(703) 777-8161
Fax: (703) 777-8157
www.willowcroftwine.com
willowine@aol.com

Windham Winery
14727 Mountain Road
Hillsboro, VA 20132
(540) 668-6464
www.windhamwinery.com
windhamwinery@hotmail.com

Wintergreen Winery
462 Winery Lane
P.O. Box 648
Nellysford, VA 22958
(434) 361-2519
Fax: (434) 361-1510
www.wintergreenwinery.com
info@wintergreenwinery.com

**Woodland Vineyard and Farm
Winery, LLC**
15501 Genito Road
Midlothian, VA 23112-5115
(804) 739-2774

Recipe Contributors

We appreciate all who graciously submitted recipes for consideration to be included in this book. We sincerely apologize if anyone's name is inadvertently missing, misspelled, or incorrectly listed.

Alpenglow Ciders
Lyda Angel
Nida Antonio
Darien Applegate
Autumn Hill Vineyards
Dianne Bailey
Sarah Bailey
Laura Bangor
Barboursville Vineyards
Linda Bawcom
Suzette BcGowen
Peggy Beale
Laura Beery
Linda Belding
Betsy Blades Belig
Gail Berra
Melanie Berra
Joy Bixler
Tricia Blair
Donna Bortell
Susan Bouffard
Mary Elizabeth Bowles
Jennifer Bowman
Breaux Vineyards
Romy Brewer
Lucy Brinkley
Denni Brown
Erin Brown
Shelly Brown
Elizabeth C. Bruce
Ann Stuart Bugg
Heidi Burnette
Burnley Vineyards
Barrett Bussard
Perry Bussard
Robin Byrd
Lisa Campbell
Meg Campbell
Shirley Carter
Courtney Castellano
Sherri Celesia
Margie Chapman
Beulah P. Chappell

Chateau Morrisette
Kim Chope
Angela Christian
Chrysalis Vineyards
Amy Cobb
Priscilla P. Coon
Cooper Vineyards
JoAnne Cotton
Mary Creekmore
Jane Currzio
Terri Darnell
Sterling Davis
Tamara Degraw
Jenn Demmin
Molly Dey
JoAnne Dickens
Stephanie Dickens
Susan Dixon
Ann Downs
Nancy Bowen Doyle
Dottie T. Dudley
Sally E. Dudley
Dye's Vineyards
Catherine Earp
Blair Ellson
Farfelu Vineyards
Jane Farmer
Rachael Feigenbaum
Grace Ferguson
Emily H. Filer
Madeline Anderson Finney
First Colony Vineyard
PJ Forbes
Marian Friske
Rebecca Frith
Gabriele Rausse Winery
Lauris Gehren
Winifred Gibbons
Cami Denison Glovier
Judith Godsey
Shelly Gram
Loretta Grant
Bobbie Gribble
Susan Gross
Jackie Hackney
Christy Hamlin
Carole Lee H. Hancock
Priscilla Hara
Janet Hare
Laurie Harrison

Sabrina Harvey
Victoria Hecht
Adeline Herman
Betty Holland
Bailey Hooten
Robert M. Hughes III
Jean D. Hughes
Gina Iavarone
Pat Iman
Ingleside Plantation Vineyard
Ford James
Jennifer James
Brad Jarrat
Constance Johnson
Kathryn Jones
Shauna M. Kale
Debbi Kaufman
Anastasia Kezman
Bettye Kight
King Family Vineyard
Kate King
Katherine Knaus
Christine Korkalo
La Provencale Cellars
Lake Anna Winery
Gray Lawson
Tracey Lee
Brenda Lindsey
JoAnne Lopes
Linda MacLaughlin
Jean Marraccini
Catherine Martin
Tracey Martin
Dana Mattocks
Robyn Maus
Abbie McBrayer
Holly McGinnis
Terra McGonegal
Carter McKay
Vicki McNamara
Cameron Meals
Margaret Merritt
Jan Meyer
Nicole Michelon
Kelly Cooper Miller
Sonja Miller
Sheila Minnich
Mobjack Bay Beer Company
Brooke M. Moffett
Kelly Mofield

Jennifer Moore
Jorj Morgan
Amy Morrissey-Turk
Sunny Mueller
Betsy Murphy
Naked Mountain Vineyard
Sue Neal
Marta Nelson
Cindy Niblo
North Mountain Vineyard & Winery
Kim Norton
Oakencroft Vineyard
Oasis Winery
Ann M. O'Driscoll
Old House Vineyards
Gina Olivieri
Mary Opitz
Sylvia Pakradooni
Beverly A. Parker
Jacqueline Peters
Louise Peters
Kirsten Peterson
Beth Phillips
Ashley Plumb
April Porter
Sheila Price
Prince Michel & Rapidan River Vineyards
Dawn Provost
Tracie Pruden
Mary Pyle
Allison Rachels
Rascona Family
Rebec Vineyards
Deborah Rice
Rockbridge Vineyard
Diane Rogic
Mike Russell
Sara M. Schroeder
Christine Scott
Margaret Seagraves
Betsey B. Selig
Kathy Shelton
Lee Walker Shepherd
Rebecca Shepherd
Cindy Sherwood
Jane Short
Melissa Siemens
Tammy Simonis

Barbara Smith
Linda Spruill
St. George Brewing
Dorothy M. Stedfast
Sarah Stedfast
Jennifer Stewart
Stonewall Vineyards & Winery
Barbara Morris Sutelan
Tarara Vineyard & Winery
Katie Teague
The Williamsburg Winery
Evelyn Thorton
Mary Ann Throckmorton
Tomahawk Mill Winery
Elizabeth Tuck
Ida Tuck
Wendy Tumlin
Charles and Francis Turgeon
Unicorn Winery
Valhalla Vineyards
Ginger VandeWater
Jennifer Vaughan
Christine Verfurth
Veritas Winery
Elizabeth Vittone
Charlotte Voight
Carolyn C. Ware
Reilly Peterson Warlick
Ilona Webb-Bruner
Melanie Weller
Laura Ann Wheeler
Anne Whipp
White Hall Vineyards
Heather White
Mrs. Gerald Glynn Williams
Williamsburg Brewing Co.
The Willliamsburg Winery
Willowcroft Farm Vineyards
Windham Winery
Rhetta Fair Wilson
Shirley T. Wilson
Lynne Winter
Wintergreen Winery
Clara Mitchell Wolcott
Anita Young
Nicole S. Zito

Test Kitchen Participants

Thanks to the dedicated test kitchen participants, the recipes in this book have been triple tested. We sincerely apologize if anyone's name is inadvertently missing, misspelled, or incorrectly listed.

Page Allard
Monica Allen
Shannon Allen
Nida Antonio
Ann Armistead
Tracy Austgen
Sarah Bailey
Yvette Baker
Anna Lee Bamforth
Linda Bawcom
Linda Belding
Melanie Berra
Joy Bixler
Karen Blackwell
Tricia Blair
Susan Bouffard
Allison Bough
Romy Brewer
Kirsten Brown
Shelly Brown
Ann Stuart Bugg
Kristan Burch
Heidi Burnette
Barrett Bussard
Mary Butler
Kathryn Callahan
Courtney Castellano
Margie Chapman
Amy Cobb
Priscilla Coon
Elizabeth Cooper
Leslie Council
Mary Creekmore
Terri Darnell
Tamara DeGraw
Francine Deir
Molly Dey
Stephanie Dickens
Susan Dixon
Mawuse Dogbe
Amy Driscoll
Sally Dudley

Catherine Earp
Ann-Stewart Ege
Blair Ege
Melissa Emerick
Ginger Faulkner
Rachael Feigenbaum
Laure Ferguson
Jennifer Fernandez
Robyn Files
Molly Flanagan
Katie Fletcher
PJ Forbes
Lauris Geheren
Cami Glovier
Julie Godwin
Shelly Gram
Angela Green
Bobbie Gribble
Kimberly Haden
Janet Hare
Pamela Harrington
Laurie Harrison
Candice Hassell
Vicky Hecht
Connie Hedrick
Christine Herbert
Michelle Hill
Bailey Hooten
Elizabeth Hutchinson
Gina Iavarone
Constance Johnson
Marla Johnson
Shann Johnson
Anastasia Kezman
Danielle Kimball
Elaine King
Kate King
Melissa King
Katherine Knaus
Christine Korkalo
Lori Krezel
Wellesley Lawrence
Laurie Leitzke
Brenda Lindsey
Joanne Lopes
Maria LoPresto
Julie MacMillan
Vickie Madison
Amy Malloy
Catherine Martin

Tracey Martin
Dana Mattocks
Robyn Maus
Terra McGonegal
Ingrid McGowan
Carter McKay
Vickie McNamara
Anne McPhee
Cameron Meals
Nicole Michelon
Caroline Minor
Kelly Mofield
Jennifer Moore
Pamela Morgan
Sarah Moriarty
Courtney Morton
Deborah Mueller
Mary Reeves Murphy
Melissa Musick
Judy Myak
Becky Neal
Marta Nelson
Cindy Niblo
Mary Opitz
Cheryl Orr
DeMonica Parker
Stacy Parker
Sarah Boxley Parrott
Ann Pavilack
Leigh Penner
Jacqueline Peters
Beth Phillips
Clenise Platt
Annette Pleasants
Ashley Plumb
April Porter
Nicole Powell
Shannon Powell
Dawn Provost
Tracie Pruden
Allison Rachels
Michele Rackard
Joan Redfearn
Heather Richardson
Beth Ripa
Elizabeth Roberts
Diane Rogic
Laura Ross
Debbie Russell
Cynthia Sabol

Michelle Schinderle
Kimberly Schrantz
Kelly Seith
Kathy Shelton
Rebecca Shepherd
Cindy Sherwood
Laura Sholes
Melissa Siemens
Cheryl Slokker
Kristina Smith
Chris Sprouse
Emily Spruill
Jennifer Stacoffe
Sherry Stein
Barbara Sutelan
Ashley Swindell
Kimberly Thompson
Eleanor Connolly Trickler
Elizabeth Tuck
Ida Tuck
Amy Morrisey-Turk
Elizabeth Upchurch
Tarrye Venable
Christine Verfurth
Elizabeth Vittone
Renee Scott Walker
Ilona Webb-Bruner
Heather White
Anne Whipp
Sarah Whiting
Celeste Whittlesey
Kelly Willette
Stacy Williams
Lynne Winter
Heather Wood
Flurry Yanez
Sabra Young
Julie Yutesler
Elizabeth Zimmerman
Astrid Zuppinger

Index

Index continued

Index continued

Index continued

Index continued

Index continued

Tips from the Testing Process

When cooking the recipes found in this book, please keep the following helpful hints in mind:

◆ Read the recipe entirely before you begin.
◆ Plan for advance preparation time if necessary.
◆ Make note of preparation and cooking times: *Preparation time* is the time it takes to get the ingredients ready before cooking. *Cooking time* is the actual amount of time the food is in the oven, on the stove, etc.
◆ Gather and arrange the ingredients in order.
◆ Follow the directions step-by-step.
◆ Check for doneness prior to time stated as temperatures may vary.
◆ Use unsalted butter.
◆ Use large eggs.
◆ Use all-purpose flour (don't sift unless directed to).
◆ Use granulated sugar unless otherwise stated.
◆ Wash and dry fresh herbs, greens, and lettuces.
◆ One teaspoon fresh herb is equivalent to ¼ teaspoon dry.
◆ Peel fresh ginger, garlic, and onions.
◆ Toasting nuts enhances their flavor. Most nuts toast in a preheated 300 degree oven for five minutes or until lightly browned. Watch carefully as they can burn quickly.
◆ When doubling recipes, start with 2/3 of spices and taste before you add more.

Glossary of Terms

◆ Dutch oven – A large, heavy pot with a tight-fitting lid so steam will not escape during cooking.
◆ Fond – Brown particles adhering to the skillet after browning or sauteeing an item. Has a lot of flavor; don't throw it out.
◆ Hard cider- Fermented apple cider usually available where liquor or wine is sold.
◆ Mirin – Japanese wine; also called rice wine. Found in the gourmet section of most grocery stores.
◆ Panko crumbs – These are Japanese bread crumbs.
◆ Paramount crystals – Flakes of oils from chocolate used to thin out the chocolate; can be found in candy supply stores.
◆ Parchment paper – A moisture-resistant paper (not wax paper) used to line baking pans. Found in gourmet stores.
◆ Roux – A mixture of butter and flour that is slightly cooked and used as a thickening agent.
◆ Smithfield Ham – To be a true Smithfield Ham, it must come from Smithfield, Virginia. This ham is dry and salty.
◆ Superfine sugar – A more finely ground sugar than granulated that dissolves faster. Granulated can be substituted equally if superfine is not available.
◆ Virginia ham – Selective fresh ham that is slowly cured, hickory smoked, glazed with sugar and spice, then oven-baked.
◆ Zest – The outer skin of a lemon, lime, or orange. Not the white, inner skin. Gadgets for easy removal of the zest from the fruit are available in gourmet stores.

Reference List

A Good Time. Any Time. City of Suffolk, Virginia. 6 Feb. 2004 < http://www.suffolk-fun.com>.

A Norfolk Treasure: Fort Norfolk. Norfolk Historical Society. 16 Oct. 2003 <http://www.norfolkhistorical.org>.

About Hampton Roads. Hampton Roads Chamber of Commerce. 6 Feb. 2004 <http://www.hamptonroadschamber.com/about_hr.php>.

About the Virginia Air & Space Center. Virginia Air & Space Center. 4 Jan. 2004 <http://www.vasc.org/generalinfo.html>.

About Us. NASA Langley Research Center. 4 Jan. 2004 <http://www.larc.nasa.gov/about_us/about_us.htm>.

About Us. Williamsburg Pottery Factory. 30 Sept. 2003 <http://williamsburgpottery.com>.

All About Suffolk. City of Suffolk, Virginia. 6 Feb. 2004 <http://suffolk.va.us>.

Anders, Barbara. *State of Mine: Tidewater, Virginia!* State of Mine. 6 Feb. 2004 <http://www.banders.com/stateofmine/tour/tidewater/tidewater.html>.

Attractions-Downtown Hampton, Virginia. Downtown Hampton Development Partnership. 29 Nov. 2003 <http://www.downtown-hampton.com/attraction.html>.

Attractions. Newport News Tourism Development Office. 19 Jul. 2003 <http://www.newport-news.org>.

Beizer, Doug. (2002, September 24). *Selling Chesapeake.* The Virginian-Pilot, pp. D1, D3.

Busch Gardens. Busch Gardens Home. 16 October. 2003 <http://www.visitwilliamsburg.com/buschgardens.htm>.

Campus Facts. College of William and Mary. 16 Oct. 2003 <http://www.web.wm.edu/about/index.php>.

Chesapeake Attractions. Chesapeake Conventions & Tourism Bureau. 30 Sept. 2003 <http://www.visitchesapeake.com/attract_chesapeake.html>.

Chesapeake, Virginia. City of Chesapeake. 19 Jul. 2003 <http://www.chesapeake.va.us/>.

The City of Norfolk. 30 Sept. 2003 <http://www.norfolk.gov>.

The City of Poquoson. 13 Sept. 2003 <http://www.ci.poquoson.va.us/>.

Cleghorn, C.W. and Allen, R.D. NASA's Langley Research Center. NASA. 12 Jan. 2004 <http://www.larc.nasa.gov/>.

Coliseum History. City of Hampton. 4 Mar. 2004 <http://www.hamptonjazzfestival.com/jazz/history.html>.

Colonial Parkway. Colonial National Historic Park. 30 Sept. 2003 <http://www.nps.gov/colo/Jamestwn/parkway.htm>.

Colonial Williamsburg. Williamsburg Area Convention and Visitors Bureau. 30 Sept. 2003 <http://www.visitwilliamsburg.com/colonial_williamsburg_foundation.htm>.

Discover Chesapeake, a comprehensive informational magazine and guide to the City of Chesapeake. City of Chesapeake. (1999-2000).

First Fighter Wing-Langley Air Force Base, Virginia. US Air Force. 12 Jan. 2004 <http://www.langley.af.mil/>.

First Landing State Park. Sunny Day Guide. 6 Feb. 2004 <http://www.sunnydayguide.com>.

Fort Monroe History. U.S. Army Training and Doctrine Command. 4 Jan. 2004 <http://www-tradoc.army.mil/museum/history.asp>.

Geocities. 1 Apr. 2004 <http://www.geocities.com/wellesley/garden/1077>.

Grymes, Charles A. *About This Site: Geography of Virginia.* George Mason University, Geography of Virginia Class (GEOG380). 7 Feb. 2004 <http://www.virginiaplaces.org/about.html>.

Reference List continued

Grymes, Charles A. *The Nine Regions of Virginia.* George Mason University, Geography of Virginia Class (GEOG380). 7 Feb. 2004 <http://www.virginiaplaces.org/regions/hampt.html>.

Grymes, Charles A. *Where Is "Tidewater" in Virginia?* George Mason University, Geography of Virginia Class (GEOG380). 7 Feb. 2004 <http://www.virginiaplaces.org/chesbay/11chesa.html>.

Guy, Louis L. (2004, January 13). *Let's Talk About a 'City of Hampton Roads'.* The Virginian-Pilot, p. B9-Local Section.

Hampton Bay Days at a Glance. Hampton Bay Days. 29 Nov. 2003 <http://www.baydays.com/glance.html>.

Hampton Jazz Festival FAQs. City of Hampton. 29 Nov. 2003 <http://www.hamptonjazzfestival.com/jazz/jazz_faqs.html>.

Hampton University-Hampton Facts. Hampton University. 3 Mar. 2004 <http://www.hamptonu.edu/about/emancipation_oak.htm>.

Hampton University-Hampton's Heritage. Hampton University. 4 Jan. 2004 <http://www.hamptonu.edu/hampton_facts/hampt_her-itage.htm>.

Hampton University-University Museum. Hampton University. 3 Mar. 2004 <http://www.hamptonu.edu/museum/index.htm>.

Hampton Roads History and Penny Postcard Tour. Historic Hampton Roads, Inc. 6 Feb. 2004 <http://www.historichamptonroads.com/>.

Hampton, Virginia Guide. BayDreaming.com. 4 Jan. 2004 <http://www.baydreaming.com/hampton.htm>.

Hampton Virginia, Fort Monroe. City of Hampton. 4 Jan. 2004 <http://www.hampton.va.us/fort_monroe.html>.

Hampton Virginia, Hampton Facts. City of Hampton. 4 Jan. 2004 <http://www.hampton.va.us/hampton_facts.html>.

Hampton Virginia/Parks/Carousel Park. City of Hampton. 29 Nov. 2003 <http://www.hampton.va.us/parks/carousel_park.html>.

HamptonRoads.com-Hampton Carousel. HamptonRoads.com/PilotOnline.com/INFOLINE. 29 Nov. 2003 <http://home.hamptonroads.com/funplaces/detail.cfm?placeID=874>.

HamptonRoads.com-Miles of Lights. HamptonRoads.com/PilotOnline.com/INFOLINE. 29 Nov. 2003 <http://home.hamptonroads.com/calendar/results.cfm>.

Haunted Virginia at All About Ghosts-Your Paranormal Portal. AllAboutGhosts.com. 5 Jan. 2004 <http://dawghouse.topcities.com/virginia.html>.

Historic and Cultural Resources Inventory. Melville Consulting Services. 15 Apr. 2003 <http://www.historicnorfolk.org>.

Historic Hampton Roads Definitions and Other Information. Historic Hampton Roads, Inc. 6 Feb. 2004 <http://www.historichampton-roads.com/Definitions.htm>.

Historic Hotels of America: The Cavalier Hotel. National Trust for Historic Preservation. 16 Oct. 2003 <http://www.nationaltrust.org/historic_hotels>.

History Guide. Virginia Beach Net. 4 Jan. 2004 <http://vabeach.com/history.htm>.

History of Bruton Parish. Bruton Parish. 12 Oct. 2003 <http://www.brutonparish.org/history.htm>.

History of Chesapeake. City of Chesapeake. 30 Sept. 2003 <http://www.chesapeake.va.us/community/about/history>.

History of Fort Monroe. U.S. Army Training and Doctrine Command. 4 Jan. 2004 <http://www.tradoc.army.mil/monroe/history.html>.

History of the Hampton Jazz Festival. City of Hampton. 29 Nov. 2003 <http://www.hamptonjazzfestival.com/jazz/history_artists.html>.

History of the Hermitage. Hermitage Foundation Museum. 16 Oct. 2003 <http://www.hermitagefoundation.org>.

History of Jubilee. Chesapeake Jubilee. 30 Sept. 2003 <http://www.chesapeakejubilee.org/pages/about.html>.

Reference List continued

History of Poquoson. City of Poquoson. 13 Sept. 2003 <http://www.ci.poquoson.va.us/history.html>.

Jamestown Settlement. Jamestown-Yorktown Foundation. 16 Dec. 2003 <http://www.historyisfun.org/jamestown/jamestown.cfm>.

Live the Life. Virginia Beach Convention & Visitors Bureau. 30 Sept. 2003 <http://www.vbfun.com>.

Location. City of Poquoson. 13 Sept. 2003 <http://www.ci.poquoson.va.us/developm.htm>.

Murphy, Morgan. (2003, Summer). *Virginia's Best Ice Cream.* Southern Living, p.2 VA.

Naval Station Norfolk Webpage. US Navy. 12 Jan. 2004 <http://www.navstanorva.navy.mil/>.

Newport News: Newcomer's Guide. Office of Intergovernmental & Community Relations. 19 Jul. 2003 <http://www.newport-news.va.us>.

Norfolk State University: Campus Facts. Norfolk State University. 19 Jan. 2004 <http://www.nsu.edu/campusfacts.nsf/pages/campusfacts>.

Northrop Grumman Corporation-Defining the Future. Northrop Grumman Corporation. 20 Sep. 2003 <http://www.northgrum.com/>.

Old Dominion University: Campus Facts. Old Dominion University. 11 Jan. 2004 <http://www.odu.edu/webroot/orgs/IA/campusfacts.nsf/pages/campusfacts>.

Official Government Website of Portsmouth, Virginia USA. City of Portsmouth, Virginia. 19 Jul. 2003 <http://www.portsmouth.va.us/>.

Parks & Facilities: Fun Forest. City of Chesapeake, Parks & Recreation Department. 30 Sept. 2003 <http://www.cityofchesapeake.net/services/depart/park-rec/fun-forest-photos.shtml>.

Poquoson, Virginia. BayDreaming.com. 13 Sept. 2003 <http://www.baydreaming.com/poquoson.htm>.

Skog, Jason. (2004, January 29). Beach Median Income is 4th Highest in U.S. The Virginian-Pilot, p. A1-Front Page.

Smithfield, Virginia: The Ham Capital of the World. Town of Smithfield. 6 Feb. 2004 <http://www.co.smithfield.va.us>.

Snead, Troy R. *Naval Air Station Oceana.* US Navy. 12 Jan. 2004 <http://www.nasoceana.navy.mil/>.

Special Deals!-Virginia Air & Space Center. Virginia Air & Space Center. 29 Nov. 2003 <http://www.vasc.org/carousel.html>.

The Chesapeake Bay Bridge Tunnel. 6 Feb. 2004 <http://www.cbbt.com>.

The Doumar Family. Doumar's. 16 Oct. 2003 <http://www.doumars.com>.

The Mission of the University. Old Dominion University. 11 Jan. 2004 <http://www.odu.edu/webroot/orgs/AO/PO/bovpols.nsf/files/1001Revised.pdf/$FILE/1001Revised.pdf>.

The New Norfolk. Norfolk Convention & Visitors Bureau. 30 Sept. 2003 <http://www.norfolkcvb.com>.

Toasting-A Memorable Art. Etiquette International. 18 April. 2003 <http://www.etiquetteintl.com/Articles/Toasting.aspx>.

TRADOC-U.S. Army Training and Doctrine Command. US Army. 12 Jan. 2004 <http://www.monroe.army.mil/>.

20th Annual Pungo Strawberry Festival. Pungo Strawberry Festival Organization. 16 Dec. 2003 <http://www.pungostrawberryfestival.org>.

23rd Annual Poquoson Seafood Festival. City of Poquoson. 13 Sept. 2003 <http://www.seafestival.com>.

Virginia Marine Science Museum. 6 Feb. 2004 <http://www.vmsm.com>.

Reference List continued

Virginia Wines. 1 Apr. 2004
<http://www.virginiawines.org/about/history2.html>.

Visit Hampton Roads Virginia. Visit Hampton Roads. 6 Feb. 2004
<http://www.visthamptonroads.com/>.

Welcome Center-Old Dominion University. Old Dominion University.
11 Jan. 2004   <http://www.odu.edu/home/welcome.html>.

Welcome to Christopher Newport University. Christopher Newport
University. 20 Sep. 2003 <http://www.cnu.edu/>.

Welcome to the City of Franklin. Franklin, Virginia. 6 Feb. 2004
<http://www.franklinva.com>.

Welcome to the City of Virginia Beach. City of Virginia Beach.
30 Sept. 2003 <http://www.vbgov.com>.

Welcome to the US Army Transportation Center and Fort Eustis, Virginia.
US Army. 12 Jan. 2004 <http://www.eustis.army.mil/>.

White, Susan E. (2004, January 3). Fit City. The Virginian-Pilot,
p.B1-Local Section.

Yorktown Victory Center. Jamestown-Yorktown Foundation. 13 Dec.
2003 <http://www.historyisfun.org/yorktown/yorktown.cfm>.

Sidebar Index

Tips on wine pairing desserts and appetizers
FARM FRESH SUPERMARKETS:

Dessert Wines

Typically one does not serve a dessert that is sweeter than the wine. The sweetness of the dessert may mask the character and finesse of the wine. Sparkling wines are generally not good marriages with dessert unless the dessert contains some fresh fruit such as strawberries or raspberries. A semi-sweet (demi-sec) style sparkling wine may sometimes marry well with lighter desserts. Other dessert style wines include late-harvest varietals such as Rieslings or Gewürztraminer or even Pinot Gris as well as late harvest Vidal wines. These wines have a richness and sweetness level that will marry with a variety of desserts. Sweet wines made from the Sauvignon Blanc and Semillon varietals also marry well with apple, pear, peach, and apricot dessert.

Wines with Appetizers

Pairing wines with appetizers is a real challenge depending on the texture and weight of each dish. Generally, one serves lighter weighted white wines that will precede more fuller bodied wines with the other courses. With seafood appetizers, a light white sparkling wine will be a good choice. The freshness and clean acidity of a top Riesling wine is often a good choice with light appetizers. As the dishes become more complex one can serve a medium bodied unoaked Chardonnay or perhaps a Viognier that has some richness but is light enough to marry with crab or scallop dishes. The grassy and herbaceous nature of the Sauvignon Blanc is a perfect match with appetizers that have a distinct herbal character.

—Professor Roy L. Williams,
ODU Wine Educator
and Farm Fresh Wine Consultant

Sponsors & Partners
A special thank you is extended to the following generous supporters.

CHAMPAGNE WITH CAVIAR – $10,000
Farm Fresh Supermarkets

MERLOT – $5000
Hampton Roads Magazine
Junior League of Norfolk-Virginia Beach, Inc. Past Presidents**
Junior League of Norfolk-Virginia Beach, Inc. Sustainers*

CABERNET – $2500
Smithfield

COMMUNITY PARTNER
United Way of South Hampton Roads

CHARDONNAY – $1000
Blue Crab Bay Company
Hubbard Peanut Company, Inc.
Pinnacle Network Systems, Inc.
San-J International, Inc.

ZINFANDEL – $500
ACS Systems
Mark Barr Companies
Jane Batten
Peggy Beale**
Citicorp Foundation in honor of Dawn Peters**
Dataline, Inc.
Heritage Wealth Management Group
Georgina Miller*
Old Dominion Peanut Corporation
Patricia Rouse**
S. L. Nusbaum Realty Company

VINTNER – $250
BJ Construction
Frank Batten, Jr.
Ed and Tricia Blair
The Honorable and Mrs. William L. Dudley, Jr.
Kaufman and Canoles
G.T. I.–Tim Miller Foundation
Virginia C. Hitch**
Kirkland Kelly**
Dawn Peters**
Jacqueline Peters**
Lisa Shapiro*
Dave and Kathy Shelton
Todd Jurich's Bistro
Anthony and Elizabeth Vittone

BEVERAGE INDUSTRY PARTNERS
Barboursville Vineyards
Cardinal Point Vineyard & Winery
Chateau Morisette
Horton Cellars Winery
King Family Vineyards
La Provencale Cellars
North Mountain Vineyard & Winery
Oakencroft Vineyard & Winery
Rockbridge Vineyard
St. George Brewing
Tarara Vineyard & Winery
The Williamsburg Winery
Wintergreen Winery

PAST PRESIDENT'S CHALLENGE PARTICIPANTS**
Sabine Andrews
Peggy Beale
Susan Bernard
Joanne Berkley
Citigroup Foundation in Honor of Dawn Peters
Molly Dey
Nancy Diffenbaugh
Emily Filer
Martha Goodman
Debra Griggs
Virginia C. Hitch
Kirkland Kelley
Glenda McKinnon
Alice McKnight
Vicki McNamara
Emily Mills
Linda Palmer
Dawn Peters
Jacqueline Peters
Martha Raiss
Patricia Rouse
Eugenia Scott
Jane Short
Helen Withers

SUSTAINER'S CHALLENGE PARTICIPANTS*
Jody Benedict
Cindy Black
Marian Breeden
Judith Brennan
Romy Brewer
Perry Bussard
Margaret Campbell
Citigroup Foundation in Honor of Dawn Peters
Betty Wade Coyle
Merilee Crocker
Gaye Deal
Mary Denny
Blair Ege
PJ Forbes
Suzanne Franklin
Marynell Gordon
Debra Griggs
Chris Hamlin
Sarah Havens
Mary Haycox
Marjorie Hill
Virginia C. Hitch
Jean Hughes
Patricia Hylton
Rachel Alfriend Jiral
Kirkland Kelley
Gwendolyn Meredith
Rexanne Metzger
Georgina Miller
Emily Mills
Elizabeth Mooz
Ann Morgan
Betsy Murphy
Pamela Panton
Dawn Peters
Jean Powell
Teresa Profilet
Margaret Ray
Robin Reeves
Paige Romig
Elizabeth Shannon
Lisa Shapiro
Lee Walker Shepherd
Elly Smith
Eleanor Snodgrass
Lynda Strickler
Suzanne Taylor
Judith Terjen
Ginger Van De Water
Betty Vansant
Jane Claytor Webster
Lauren Wolcott

Order Form

Sold to:

Name _____

Address _____

City _____ State _____ Zip _____

Daytime Phone Number (_____) _____ Evening Phone Number (_____) _____

E-mail address _____

Ship to: (If different from "Sold To" address) _____

Name _____

Address _____

City _____ State _____ Zip _____

Method of Payment

_____ Check *(made payable to: JLNVB)*

_____ VISA   _____ MasterCard

Name as it appears on card _____

Card Number _____

Expiration Date _____ 3-Digit Security Code (found on back of card) _____

Signature _____

Please send me:

_____ copies of *Toast to Tidewater* $27.95 each $ _____

_____ copies of *Tidewater on the Half Shell* $18.95 each $ _____

Prices subject to change without notice.

Virginia Residents add 5% sales tax:

Toast to Tidewater $1.40 each $ _____

Tidewater on the Half Shell $ .95 each $ _____

Subtotal $ _____

Shipping: $5 for first book and $2 per additional book $ _____

Gift Wrapping (optional): $3 per book $ _____

If gift, enclosure card to read: _____

Total enclosed $ _____

Thank you for your order.

Proceeds from the sale of our publications support the mission and programs of the Junior League of Norfolk-Virginia Beach, Inc.

Please photocopy, complete this form, and mail it to:

JUNIOR LEAGUE OF NORFOLK-VIRGINIA BEACH

Women building better communities

Post Office Box 956
Norfolk, VA 23501
(866) 905-5682
Phone: (757) 623-7270
Fax: (757) 623-3932
www.jlnvb.org

THE JUNIOR LEAGUE OF
NORFOLK-VIRGINIA BEACH, INC.

An Overview

In 1925, Mrs. Lawrence F. Tucker formed the Junior League of Norfolk with ten charter members. Their first community service was providing transportation to city agencies.

Today, the Junior League of Norfolk-Virginia Beach, Inc. (JLNVB) continues to deliver much-needed community support through its services and grants. The JLNVB has provided more than $725,000 in direct grants to various community organizations, ranging from cultural (Academy of Music) and educational (Literacy Project PALS) to social welfare (F.O.R. Kids, Inc.) and healthcare (EDMARC Hospice for Children).

The JLNVB has nearly 200 active members and close to 300 sustaining members. Our association is rooted in the belief that a group of women can be a powerful force for change. The League offers women the opportunity to implement change in their communities and connect with other women who are similarly concerned for our present and future generations.

The JLNVB is committed to promoting voluntarism, developing the potential of women, and improving communities through effective action and leadership of trained volunteers. Its purpose is exclusively educational and charitable.